A
ROAD TRIP
with a
PSYCHIC

Karen N Sawyer

2

CONTENTS

PREFACE

This is not going to be like one of those long-running daily soap operas! You know the ones I'm talking about, the ones where you can miss a decade or two, as I've done by the way, and still catch up with the next episode. Anyone who laughs, here, hasn't watched daytime TV! Well, my life hasn't been a soap opera, although it has certainly been interesting. It has had more ups and downs than I'd like to remember, especially from the prospective of hindsight. Hindsight is the flipside of foresight, which is what psychic really means. You know beforehand, so you can make changes or do something another way – an easier way – before you fall down the hole of a really bad choice... and we've all had at least one of those, right?

The reasons I decided to write this book were simple.

By using the psychic threads of my life as a backdrop, I hope to show how we've all been given a set of tools to work with, and to weave our way through the life we've chosen. I feel it is important to make sure you're aware of all the tools at your disposal, and not just the physical ones you can see, hear, taste, touch, and feel. I mean the ones that take a little more exercise, to get them working for you. Once they do, you can enjoy a life full of the promise you came here with and the one you so wanted to fulfill... until – maybe – life got in the way.

I want to help others to understand and expand on these tools – these gifts – if they choose to do so. These *psychic gifts* begin with learning to understand your intuitive side. Learning how it can really help you throughout your life. Understanding that being psychic doesn't just apply to other people. I want to help you to see that psychics are normal people. We have our highs and lows just as you do, and – just like us – you have a psychic intuitive sense within you.

I want to show you how you can learn to access and use your intuition just as I did. Just as I've learned to use my intuition, over the years, to help me understand WHY and HOW, and to understand myself better. I gained a better view, if you will, of all that has happened to me. I will tell you how I learned to transform my perspective, from a negative to a positive one, and this guided me from a place of pain and self-doubt to a place of healing and self-empowerment. I also found that the more I helped others the more I learnt about myself in the process. What I came to understand is this; we all want to get rid of self-doubt and to feel more confident in our lives. The way to do this is to begin trusting in you. I can show you a way to do this.

I can help you learn to use your intuition as I did. It can help you make better choices for yourself, which – if you, if we – allow, will start the creation of a more fulfilling life. And, this won't just be for yourselves, but will also have a flow-on effect in the lives of your children, loved ones, and friends around you. What is important is what you do with the knowledge you have.

Whatever you discover and decide to use, during our time together, is up to you. During this time, you will learn about my fears, and you may see what I used to think of as my failures, but I promise you this! You and I are going to have a lot of fun along the way. All I ask is that you keep an open mind, because I AM just like you.

This book came to be, because I was looking for a way to keep all the thoughts and ideas I've had, in one place, without having to hunt around for the pieces of paper I write my poems, and notes on; the bits and pieces of my life that I put to paper all the time. Yes, guilty as charged. I still actually **LOVE** ♥ writing on paper. I'm just a lot faster on a keyboard and at least I can read it back, which is always a plus.

By the time, I got my notes onto my computer (and there were so many of them!) I had started to think that maybe they could help others just as they've helped me, along the way.

Apart from wanting to try to help others, there is another important reason. I wanted to have something of me that will not perish, like my notes that were put out in the recycling. I wanted something tangible that represented me. Me, in the way I think, the way I feel and the things I find funny. This spirit, who is me, and who resides in this physical body for whatever time I have in this plane of existence. I wanted something of substance that my children and grandchildren could hold, and know that not only did it help others (I hope) but that they hold the heart of who I truly am. I wanted this more than anything else, so that my family can feel they still have the most important part of me with them, my heart and soul, my truth.

So that when you read this my darlings, you will recognise me. And, you will know that you have my heart always and forever, without conditions! I feel the best gift I can give you is to for you to truly know who your mother was – and well, is – because I'm not actually planning to go anywhere anytime; within the next few decades... at least!!!

*****

This is my story, my perceptions, my feelings, and my understanding. You may find you resonate to some of these, or none of them, and that's okay. Our feelings belong to no one else. We all have our own histories and they colour our emotions and the feelings that grow from them. We are all unique; therefore, our feelings are unique to us, as well. Some similar patterns may arise for you and you may feel connected to some of these. If you do, I hope my story can help you with at least some of them.

Now, everyone knows that the joy of a road trip comes from the detours and diversions, the things that throw you off course and off balance. These are some of the things that make life interesting, and I can't deny that my life has been interesting.

And so, to begin.

However, to do that, I must take you back to when it all began for me. Are you ready?

I was 17 years old and it was the day of Poppy's funeral...

"Our job in this lifetime

is not to shape ourselves into some ideal

we imagine we ought to be,

but to find out who we already are

and become it."

Wayne W. Dyer 2016

CHAPTER 1

Funerals and the Spirits that Don't Die

I know there are many psychics/mediums who 'just knew' they had their gifts from a young age and used them. Not me! Although, looking back from here, I can see that there were many times where it was so obvious. Then, it really didn't seem a big deal to be able to feel when someone had died, to hear the phone ring before it actually did, or to know who was there without being told.

I guess you could call me a slow learner, or maybe I was just preoccupied with the growing up stuff. All of that changed on the day of my poppy's funeral. However, before I get into that, I would like to share a little about myself, and my relationship with my poppy.

I started ballroom dancing at the age of thirteen. My first public appearance was in front of my poppy at a club. My partner walked me over to curtsey in front of him, before we started.

He was so shocked and so happy, as we looked at each other. Then I danced for him. I had never felt more proud than I did in that moment. We had such a special bond, made strong since Nana died and Poppy sold their home and moved in with us. I was about three at that time and he used to teach me nursery rhymes.

My favourite nursery rhyme was Jack and Jill. One night, when Dad came home from work, I recited it to him. My poppy had taught me a second verse that he knew.

When I started with "Noo, that story's naught quit t'rue…," my dad said, "What's going on here, Pop? I've got another little Cockney in the house!" You see Poppy was born in England. He came here years later, with the family he had created, but he never lost his cockney accent. I've always loved those special memories of my poppy and I. Maybe this is why he chose to let me know he was still around and stayed around for me after he passed. He most certainly was the start of a journey, although I would not begin it in earnest, until my early forties.

My partner and I had been at dancing practice, which we had four nights a week. Dad came to the front door the minute I reached up to knock. He must have seen me arriving. We went inside and he asked me to come and sit down in the lounge room. He told me that poppy had died of a heart attack, while holidaying in Perth with his second wife. Dad said the funeral would be the following week, after all the arrangements had been made, although I wasn't really listening as tears trickled down my face. I went to my bedroom and cried until I fell asleep.

I worked the next day. In my lunch hour, I walked around the city as I always did, but nothing felt the same. Everything seemed pointless. I felt as if I had lost my best friend in the whole world and it would never be the same – and it wasn't. How could it be? The week leading up to poppy's funeral seemed endless. At least he went out having fun, I told myself, when my grief threatened to overwhelm me. Humour was to became a tool I used to deflect pain or grief whenever they became too much. It was a small comfort only, but it helped with the deep sense of loss I felt at Poppy's passing.

We didn't have a church service, as my family were not churchgoers. At that time, I had not been to church for five years. I was exactly twelve years old, when I was kicked out of Sunday School. Well, not exactly *kicked out*, but told by the minister to leave and "Seriously, think about whether this is the best place for you?" Apparently, I asked too many questions and kept interrupting his lessons. I was never one for taking things at face value. After I left church, I decided to look around for something else and I found Elvis!

"My religion is kindness"
Dalai Lama

Poppy was to be cremated at Rookwood Cemetery in Sydney. Back in those days, crematoriums were not as user-friendly as they are now, and it was a terrifying experience for me. My pop had lived with us for many years. He was the first person, whom I felt really close to, who had died, and I loved him more than words. We were ushered into the crematorium where there were long wooden benches for us to sit on.

The room was completely austere. I remember the walls were white. It was very bright, and not at all what I expected, but then I hadn't really expected anything, if you know what I mean. The room just felt strange and cold. I sat in the front row with my parents and my younger brother and sister. The wooden coffin was right there, like a huge white elephant, silent but speaking volumes with its inescapable presence. I remember feeling really nervous, and so sad and empty. The only other thing I remember about the service was when they pushed the button.

The door at the end of the conveyor belt, on which Poppy's coffin was sitting, opened and he started to slide away from me. I watched him, pulling away from us, from me, and heading towards the dark cavity that had opened up in the wall ahead. I heard someone screaming... "No! No!"

It must have been me, because I felt my father's arms around me, pulling me back, and holding me to his chest, while my poppy disappeared forever.

That memory has stayed with me my whole life, but the pain attached to it has faded over time, as it does. The memory also served me well when I began work as a funeral director, a few years ago. I loved this work more than anything I had ever done and my earlier experience with my poppy helped me to empathise with the families. I was also able ease some their fears about the crematorium service, and to soothe and dispel many of the apprehensions for the families I guided through the process. But, that's another story; one I'll tell you about a bit later.

I was also very grateful for my lack of *influenced knowledge*, back then, which allowed me just to accept what happened next with childlike innocence and trust, even although I was seventeen, and as such thought I knew everything there was to know already.

After the service had finished we were standing outside in the rose garden, when my mother said, "Come honey and I'll show you where Poppy is going to go." She took my hand and led me to a beautiful garden. "He will be here, right beside your nana, so they can be together again, forever." *My Nana had died 15 years earlier, when I was not quite two. Although I can still remember her in life, quite vividly, I have no recollection of her death.*

Standing beside my mother, I heard what she said, but when we turned to walk away, I knew it wasn't true, because he – his spirit – hitched a ride back home with us. Poppy told me he was with Nana, now. He told me that he had left as soon as he had passed over.

"You didn't die?" I asked.

Poppy said that everyone believes different things about death and dying, but he just felt a really sharp pain in his chest, and then he fell asleep. When he woke up Nana was there with him and they are so happy to be together, again.

"I miss you so much Poppy."

"Just whispe' me name, Luv. If you eve' need me. I'll be fere." Of course, no one else in the car heard or even knew about this, but I was okay with that and just being able to talk to my pop throughout the following years helped me a lot.

*****

As I mentioned earlier, I was a funeral director for a few years and I loved that job. It seemed to be made for me and I was certainly pointed in that direction by my intuition. To explain, one Saturday night, my children were going to a birthday dinner at the Brighton le Sands Novotel. I had a couple of hours before I had to pick them up and drive us home. I drove into the city and met a girlfriend. We went to an art show. The funny thing was that, because of this, I had to drive past a huge billboard on the road I took, near the airport. I drove by not once but twice, so I had little chance of missing it.

It was advertising a funeral brand. Now, it had only been there for a month and if it hadn't been for that birthday dinner, I probably would never have seen it. I had never even thought about becoming a funeral director, during my working life, but this billboard was huge and something about it stuck with me. A week later, I was going on a working holiday, to attend a seminar in Mexico, so my mind was full of travel details and the like. However, the following Monday, I noticed a branch of that same funeral service company, as I was driving home. I turned around and, as the office was still open, I parked my car and walked across the road to knock on the front door. At this point I was not thinking. I was only doing what I felt compelled to do.

I woman came out and I asked if she knew if they were hiring any new people. We talked for about twenty minutes and she gave me a contact number, which I called the next morning. An interview was arranged for that afternoon and then a physical assessment on the following day, a Wednesday. I didn't work at my job on either of those days. Two days later, I received a call offering me a role as a funeral director. We agreed on a start date and they said they would email me the details.

The point I want to make here, is that my intuition was quite literally giving me not only signs but BILLBOARDS, to guide me into the next phase of my life. I was apparently not going to miss this opportunity. If I had stopped to second guess what was happening, I probably wouldn't have even given it another thought. If I had, then I would have placed it in the too hard basket. *I know you've got one too, so you'll get it* – and then I would have looked at it again when I returned from Mexico. But, that would have been too late. Timing is everything and if it is meant for you, you need act on the signs immediately. Otherwise, you might miss a fantastic opportunity that was actually yours... but was given away to someone else who did act on it... on the signs that were in their face.

I was happy in the job I already had, but, when your intuition practically yells out a new direction, moving forward, and taking the steps I needed to take, didn't feel strange, it felt seamless. There were no stops signs. There were only green lights ahead and I didn't feel I needed to make a decision. I had made that at some other time in some other space. I stepped straight into the flow and it was amazing.

I remember the first service I went to, in training, which was a three-month process.

My trainer, Sienna, told me, "Karen I need to go and get the coffin in place for the service. You don't have to, but if you feel you can, could you come and help me?"

I thought about it for a moment, I had only been in training for a week and I had never seen a dead body before.

"Yes I'd like to."

I would be crazy to go through all the training only to find out, in three months' time, that I wasn't able to cope with seeing a dead body. We left the office and proceeded through the chapel to help get the deceased ready for his service. It was to be an open coffin service.

We put the coffin in place in the chapel, and put the lid in the corner before we began getting him ready for his service, his family, and all the people he'd loved, and who had loved him. As we were doing this, I saw the spirit of the man who had passed. He was standing in the corner watching us. He was smiling at me. He looked very happy, cheeky, and debonair all at once. Of course, I couldn't speak to him in front of Sienna. She wouldn't have understood.

About a week later, we were back at the same funeral home and I was looking at an Order of Service on the manager's desk. I was reading the back page when she said, "That's the man whom you helped get ready last week, Karen."

"No," I said, "it can't be, He looked nothing like this." I remembered him the way I had seen him outside his coffin, not inside lying down in it.

"Yes it is. He had a terminal illness and was very sick for a long time. His family said it was a blessing when he finally left them."

Then I really looked over the Order of Service, and at all the photos of him during his life. This information helped and prepared me, more than anything else did, during my training period for the role I was about to commence. Not that the manager or any of the other girls knew, and especially not Sienna. I came to understand that the spirit I had seen was the essence of this beautiful man and who he was, vibrant and living a full and happy life. I had seen peace, joy, and love in his face. It was no longer held in the pain-filled earthly body that he had once inhabited, here on earth.

About a month later, Sienna and I were talking about our previous jobs and it turned out that we had met a few years ago, at the football, in a lounge I was working in at the time. She had been in advertising and the agency she worked for had taken a private box; the one I worked in, for one of the Sunday games.

"What did you do in the lounge?" she asked. "I don't remember you."

"It was a long time ago there is no reason why you should" I told her, realising I needed to get off this subject if I had any chance of keeping my secret, but she wouldn't let it go.

I could see her mind ticking over, then suddenly she said..." Oh my God, Karen! That was you? What on earth possessed you to do this?"

"I never really thought it through that far I was just following my instincts, my intuition at the time and I'd really rather you didn't use that term around me." I replied.

"What term?" she asked.

"You know, possessed."

She looked at me for a minute and then she burst out laughing. I also started laughing at the absurdity of the whole situation.

"Sienna, you can't tell anyone, they wouldn't understand and I already love this job."

"You do know you're crazy, Karen."

"Yes, I've been told that many times. If it doesn't bother you, it doesn't bother me."

Sienna just shook her head then wanted to know if I had seen anything during my time with her.

"What do you think?" I laughed. Then I shared a couple of things with her, and we never spoke of it again.

*****

If I needed proof that life goes on after death, I certainly fell into the best job in the world. This role was an incredible gift and honour for me to perform. It taught me about the diversity of cultural belief systems, and how similarly and differently we all say goodbye before we send our loved ones off to a better life. It taught me about the different ways each of us processes grief. Never did I witness a spirit who wasn't happy in death and didn't want to go... I should say wasn't ready to go over. Although there are some exceptions. I talk about one such exception later, a woman living on a property in Picton.

*****

I've been witness to many funeral services, ones I've arranged, and ones I've been called in to attend, that is, the service of another funeral director. It was during one of those that I saw something that made my heart sing and tears of happiness rush to my eyes.

A woman's husband had passed away and I watched her sitting in the front row as the service honouring her husband's life went on. She looked so sad and frail, and my heart filled with love for her. I always loved listening to the eulogy, and learning about the deceased's life. This couple loved dancing. The family member, who was speaking, described how dancing was such a big part of their lives. As always, I was standing at the back of the church or chapel.

Towards the end of the service, and just as the final piece of music began telling the mourners that it was time to leave, I saw her husband's spirit come out from behind the curtains. He walked over to his wife, stood before her, bowed, and extended his hand for her to dance with him. I watched in wonder and awe, as her spirit rose, and he took her in his arms. I watched as they danced. In that moment, *I felt their love and I knew* they would be together again, very soon. No words can describe the gratitude and humility I felt in being gifted the witnessing of that moment.

Sometimes, I was able to witness what it meant to be not just life partners but also true spiritual partners. It always made my heart soar. Being professional is extremely important, but I felt so overwhelmed that I had to step outside to get my emotions under control. This was the most beautiful thing I've ever witnessed. A love that goes beyond the grave can only be imagined by those of us who are still mortal. To bear witness to the depth of this kind of love is a gift I will treasure always.

*****

I received a phone call from a dear friend of mine, Jane, asking if I could help someone she knew, who had a ghost living in her house. Apparently, this ghost was scaring her two boys. I asked her to try a couple of things and let me know if it helped.

The following day I received another call saying, "It's still there in the house. Is there any way you could come down and have a look around?"

"I'm not working tomorrow," I replied. "If you let me know what time you'll be home, I can drive down to Picton, meet you at yours and we can drive out to her place together."

"Oh thanks Karen, she is really beside herself."

We arranged a time and I drove down the following day. On the drive down, I received a message about the woman, so I knew who was still living in their house and why. Once we arrived, Hope came out to the gate to meet us, and my girlfriend introduced us. We walked inside her home and Hope showed us where she always felt the ghost, which was mainly in her sons' rooms. Her sons were in their late teens and early twenties, and not the kind of boys that scared easily.

She said, "This has them really rattled and with my husband away so much for work I'm actually feeling scared now too."

I explained, "The lady still living here is not harmful. She thinks that your boys are her children. She is only trying to look after them. All we need to do is let her know that her boys are on the other side and have been waiting for her to come back to them. It might take a bit to get her into the light, as her energy feels quite solid, but don't worry. We will help her together. She has been here for a very long time, since the 1930s, I'm getting."

As we walked through each room, I could feel that her energy was strongest in the lounge. That would be the room we would use to call her into the light. I don't know how other psychics or mediums clear out energies that don't belong, but I like to create a sacred circle. It took her – the ghost... while, as she was very stubborn and it was hard getting her to listen. However, once she understood that her children had died a long time ago, and that they were waiting for her on the other side, she eventually left. I took a walk around the inside of the house and then outside, to make sure I couldn't feel her energy anymore. Two huge dogs walked with me, as backup, I guess.

A few weeks later Hope's husband called to thank me. He had been worried about not being there, but said they could all tell she was gone, and the house had a great feel to it now.

*"The magic in the mystery of death
is that none of us truly know,
until our own time is near."*

CHAPTER 2

The Psychic

Time passed, I grew up, and dancing was still my life. We trained every night, and helped out in the studio on Monday nights. There was a big dancing event coming up and we decided to have a fundraiser to help hire a bus for transportation. That fundraiser was where I first came into contact with a real psychic, well almost.

My partner was Roman Catholic and he didn't believe in anything other than his religion, and I understood that. What I didn't understand was why he forbade me to go and see her, as some of my girlfriends were. I was crushed, but I did as he asked because it seemed less hassle.

My Pop being around had become normal to me, but something stopped me from telling anyone – not even my sister, and especially not my partner, who had met him before he died. Although, somewhere during the past seven or eight years I'd stopped talking to Pop and he wasn't really around much anymore. I put this down to life in general. I was growing up, and moving on with my life. I didn't really need him as I used to and that was okay. This seemed normal, too.

My sister was really angry that I hadn't seen the psychic as I had wanted to and suggested we go to an appointment by ourselves.

"We can take notes for each other," she said. Now, I was the one who was nervous. What my sister was suggesting would make my partner furious if he ever found out.

"So why does he have to find out?" she asked as if reading my mind. I started to wonder, I mean, could they really do that? I had heard that some people really believed in that kind of stuff. Others swore they were just saying what you wanted to hear and taking your money.

Well, my sister is nothing if not persistent, so one day when she met me for lunch, she said, "Come on, Sis. I've booked you in with a psychic, so we'd better hurry."

With that, she grabbed my hand and practically dragged me down the street. I was too dumbfounded to protest. She stopped outside the Dymocks building on George Street, Sydney. "I thought they only deal in books," I said.

"That's on the ground floor. We're going up to the fourth," she said. "Come on, hurry up. You don't want to be late. She's fantastic! I had a reading with her last week."

We got out of the lift, walked down the hall and went into a small office. The psychic's name was Freya. She welcomed us, and then she took me behind a curtained-off area where we sat down. My sister sat just outside on a chair with the notebook she'd bought to record what was said. Today you can record things with your smart phone, and I always suggest to my clients that they do this, if they want to.

Although I didn't disbelieve, I thought to myself; if she is just good at guessing things by reading facial expressions and body language then I am going to make her work for it. I promised myself I would not react to anything she said.

Throughout the whole half hour, I sat stony-faced, unblinking, and giving nothing away. However, Freya knew things about me. Things I had only ever though about. She knew about decisions I had made about my life, and things I'd never told a soul, not even my sister. The main thing was that I was going to see a psychologist. This was something to hide back then, and I certainly felt ashamed that I couldn't move forward without needing some help, but I didn't want anyone to know. Thankfully, times are different now.

The psychic knew these things; not all of them, but enough so that from that day on, I absolutely believed there really were people who could see and hear more than the rest of us. I still didn't think of myself in those terms. Talking to my pop was one thing, but I hadn't yet made the leap to..." Is it possible I can also do what she does?"

I could, although not exactly the same way and not until many years later. Actually, it wasn't until after my father died, when I was in my early forties, that I began to accept that I had a gift to contribute. It really was for me and it still is. Being able to communicate between worlds, and to offer what help I can to those, who seek me out, has been so rewarding and has taught me a lot about the human condition and myself.

But, I'm getting a little ahead of myself...

*****

I did a lot of acting during my 20s. Life was not how I had imagined it would be and while I always tried to appear happy on the outside, I kept my true self to myself and felt hermit-like and isolated most of the time. However, if you stay in the cave too long, pretending, you run the risk of allowing love and life in all its beauty, colours, shapes, and sizes to pass you by. This is when I started seeing Dr. Hensley. He worked in an old building on the corner of a main intersection in Bondi Junction. Here, I first learned about meditation and it was where I first astrally travelled; and no one was more surprised than I was. It happened during my last appointment.

The first day I went to see Dr. Hensley he waved me to a seat in his office. After he took down my details, he asked me to tell him why I was there. No one had ever really asked me a question about me before, so when I started speaking, all the pain that I had been feeling poured out along with a description of what my life had been like over the past, maybe ten years. After twenty minutes or so, he stopped me.

He said, "Karen, I have heard everything you've just told me. Now I have one question to ask you. Why don't you think you deserve to be happy?" Time slowed right down, all my feelings subsided, and I looked at him

"I don't know," I said. No one had ever asked about my happiness before.

Then he said, "Okay, well why don't we try and find out here together?"

"Alright" I answered, nodding my head.

I realised I had built my whole life around being *small*, about hiding in plain sight, and being invisible to others. I had lost myself before I had ever had the chance to discover who I was or what I might become.

A big part of this discovery meant accepting and embracing my sixth sense, my psychic abilities. After I acknowledged this, I was able to access the deepest part of myself, my soul. In a way, it helped me to understand why I had *hidden* myself for all of this time; I did it for self-protection.

I felt everything too deeply: the energy around and within me, and others. The laughter and the happiness, but mostly the pain and tears. There were many tears. I carried it all with me because of innocence and naivety. Beginning therapy with Dr. Hensley was the beginning of my learning how to get myself back to a place of feeling happiness within and around me. Each week, I discovered a little bit more about not only who I was but also who I wanted to be.

I remember our last session so vividly. We did a meditation practice. I'd never done one before, and I didn't even know what it was. Because of that, I was completely open to it and by now (after four months), I trusted Dr. Hensley implicitly. He felt a bit like my grandfather, but not, obviously. This is where I learnt the value of meditation. (Although we *know* something is good for us, it doesn't necessarily follow that we will do it.)

I was sitting in a comfortable chair and feeling very relaxed. Then, he started.

"Now I want you to close your eyes, Karen, and take a deep slow breath, in and out, in and out. Feel yourself relaxed and comfortable. I want you to feel how light your body is. I want you to feel yourself rising up out of the chair and floating up higher and higher until you can touch the ceiling. Now keep rising up through the ceiling and out into the open air, rising high above this building.

There are no barriers. You can see everything. I want you to look down and see the top of the roof and the colour. I want you to look at the cars moving along the road. See their colours and as you look above you note the colour of the sky and if there are any clouds..."

"Alright now, it's time to start coming back, Karen. I want you to slowly descend, coming back down through the roof and down into this room, until you can feel yourself softly sitting back into the chair below you."

All this was very nice and relaxing and I get it, you keep visualising and I was. Right up until I hit the chair with such force that my eyes flew open. I was shaking and not sure exactly what had just happened to me.

"What was that?"

I was stunned as Dr. Hensley explained about astral travelling.

"Whoa... can I do that again?" I asked.

He laughed.

"Anytime you want, Karen, but we need to put a few precautions in place first. Maybe to start with, imagine you're attached to your body with a long silver cord that can stretch forever. That way you will know that you can always get back when you want to. I'd suggest short trips until you feel ready."

"Okay." I said. "That was amazing!" I realised much later on, that this was just another stepping-stone on my travels to my true purpose.

The more I learnt, the more I grew, and sometimes being *psychic* didn't help. Sometimes it left me feeling more confused than ever, when my so-called predictions changed direction mid-stream.

Then, it made sense to me that there were those, who didn't believe in the power of psychic prediction. However, the more I learned and tested myself, the more I began to understand prediction is a fluid thing. This is because it is about energy, and energy is fluid. Just because something is right, right now, does not mean it will be in *the future*.

The future is only a construct; a projection of where we want to go, or hope we will go. The truth is that everything can only be true in the moment of its conception. Energy, my thoughts, and your thoughts can all change. If or when they do, you or I may have inadvertently set a different course for ourselves, which may or may not cancel out what was true earlier. However, if we stay the course of our original thoughts and the energy attached to them, well – anything is possible, if you believe it is.

We all come here with our purpose clear, and shining brightly for all to see. Clear, clean, visible spirits are filled with the knowledge of self-love. Each one of us is a vessel and within that vessel lies the reality of who we are. A divine expression of pure love resides within all living beings.

Part of this is why we love babies and want to be around them so much. Their eyes, their mouths, and their faces are an open expression of pure love, and pure spirit. As they grow towards their rightful place, we – as impure spirits – try to tame then into conforming. We are their teachers and, although we try to teach them, we must be willing to listen and to learn from them, as they share their knowledge with us. Broken spirits are the result of the crushing blows that are delivered by those who don't understand, or have been hurt and humiliated for expressing their true self.

When spirit is the master and life its driver, many things, and course changes can happen. My many course changes have taught me this; *when Spirit is the master and Spirit the driver, all things in your imagination are real and held in possibility. If you can think it, you can be it, and you can create it.*

Life is our ego saying "you can't do that, don't strive too high you won't make it." Don't give your ego a voice! Life puts many obstacles in our path, and dares us to feel confident enough to keep moving forward, with a heartfelt knowledge of our purpose. This knowledge speaks to you through your intuition and your psychic knowledge.

When the soul speaks out, silencing your fears, those who hear her voice rejoice in the knowledge that the time has come to express your inner self, your inner voice, for this is the heart's longing of a single soul's journey. The time has come when purpose is acknowledged, exposed, and accepted. Now your journey begins in truth and all the lessons in life mean nothing unless the voice is bathed in light.

*****

We know that some people can swim faster than we can, run faster than we can, play music better than we can, ski better than we can, and whatever it is, do it better than we can. Thus, is it so much of a stretch for us to then open our minds up to the possibility that there are others out there who can hear more than we can, see things more clearly than we can and who feel things more deeply than we do?

Why do you think this is? One, it is because they have an aptitude for what they do, what they are drawn to do, and what they were born to do. Two, it is because they put more time into doing what they do, because they love what they do. For them, this is their purpose.

Whether we know it yet or not, we all have an aptitude for being and fulfilling our purpose.

Take a moment right here, right now. Close your eyes, take a deep, deep breath and exhale. Do it again, a couple more times. Can you feel how much peace, and how much silence you feel when the focus goes within? From this space within, imagine... allow your feelings to connect to secrets, your secret longings deep within this space that you created. Feel the feeling, voice it aloud. Tell your ears what they need to hear... your heart's longing...

When something fills your whole being with heartfelt passion, it makes you want to devote as much time to it as possible and to learn and strive to be better at it. When passion meets purpose, magic becomes real. We can now look at being psychic in another way. It is not so different from any other vocation. An intangible energy pulls and guides you towards it, and keeps you studying, training, and learning because it excites and fills you from within. This is your purpose. You see; we're not so different you and I.

I remember watching an interview some years back given by John Edward, a well-respected Psychic Medium from America, after he had done a show giving readings to people in the audience. The interviewer asked him "Why do you always talk so fast when you do your readings?" I cannot remember what he said exactly because I was thinking about the question.

Even though it just happens like that, I really wanted to understand why it did and I came to understand it this way. When words are coming through for someone, they are coming *through* my mind but not *from* my mind. There is no thought process involved on my part. It is a direct connection with the spirit and the information they want to give to the person with me. It also has to do with the rising of my vibration and the lowering of spirit's, so a connection can be made. It is a strange feeling to know that I am speaking, but nothing of what I am saying is mine or is coming from me.

You may or may not want to be a psychic. Who am I to judge one way or the other? What I do know, for certain, is that learning the basics of how to start trusting my intuition was the beginning of my finding my way back to my real self again. Being psychic has also taught me that every *single person can do this*. They just need to trust and believe they can. They also have to want to try. It may not be your vocation, but it might be one of the tools that lead you to it.

Moving forward in life means you must begin by believing in yourself, and by knowing that no one else can do it for you. As psychics, mediums, clairvoyants, or whatever gift we have, we can certainly help you. We love helping others and sometimes we all need this *short cut* to help us. However, learning to trust, believe, and know, *without a doubt*, that you can act upon your own intuition is exactly the place to begin the best gift you can give yourself.

"There is no need to seek out others when you have the confirmation you need within your own heart."

CHAPTER 3

Matt, Mona and Me

Have you ever felt as if you've been given a glimpse of your future? I have, although I only knew that from the perspective of hindsight.

It was the year I met Matt. We had only been together for two weeks, when Christmas came and I was supposed to travel up to Queensland with my sister for a two week holiday. I was thinking about Matt and how we had said goodbye, the night before, as we got into her car to leave.

His demeanour had rattled me a little. He didn't want me to go, which was quite understandable, but the feeling I got was something more. It just didn't sit well with me. It felt as if he was telling me I couldn't go away from him, and when he grabbed my arms and kissed me goodbye, it felt more like a punishment than a sweet 'goodbye I'll miss you' kind of kiss.

"I'll be back in two weeks, it's not that long," I said to him as I quickly walked back to my car.

"Hey, Sis, where are you? Come on get in. We've got a long drive home. I want to get out of Sydney, before the traffic gets too heavy," said my sister. She hit the accelerator and the car took off, heading north. The niggly feeling I'd had disappeared and I didn't give Matt a moment's thought after that. My sister and I had a great time; we always did. We crashed at home that first night, ordered in, watched a movie, and then went off to bed. The weather was always perfect whenever I was there on holidays.

While away at my sister's, I decided not to venture into a relationship with Matt. I had been thinking about him a couple of days before I was to fly back to Sydney. I couldn't put my finger on it, but in some ways I didn't feel he was being honest, and while I was away from him, I didn't miss him at all and I felt great. My feeling so good, without him, gave me a point of reference and it made me question why?

Another sign for me were the movies my sister and I went to see, two nights before I flew home. It was a double feature and Michael Douglas starred in both. The movies were 'Fatal Attraction' and 'War of the Roses'. I'm sure most people have heard of 'Fatal Attraction'. A married man has an affair that goes horribly wrong. The 'War of the Roses' was about a married couple who fought constantly, to the point where their relationship became extremely violent. To say it didn't end well is a huge understatement, with their house quite literally crumbling around them.

I should have put these insights/feelings together, however I didn't. It was very clear to me that by seeing him again I was going against all the 'signs' my intuition had pushed in front of me. So, why was I ignoring them? I think this was made clear to me a week after I arrived back home. My girlfriend was having a BBQ at her house in the eastern suburbs of Sydney.

"Bring the new boyfriend," she said, "I want to get a look at him."

"I'm not too sure I'm going to keep seeing him, but for God's sake don't say that to him," I said.

She promised she wouldn't. "I just wanted to see if he is right for you."

Matt and I drove over to her place that Saturday and I introduced him to everyone. Matt seemed to be fitting in well. We were all sitting around laughing and having a drink when Matt pulled me onto his lap.

"What are you doing?" I asked.

The next moment he shouted out to everyone, "Hey guys I'm going to marry this woman and have babies with her!"

I nearly choked on my drink. My girlfriend looked daggers at me, as though I'd kept a secret from her. I was still in shock and dumbfounded, but everyone else was busy congratulating us. I couldn't do anything, but put a weak smile on my face... didn't want to embarrass him in front of everyone, so I kept my mouth shut. I told Matt I was going down to help out in the kitchen, to get away for a bit.

"Okay give, why didn't you tell me you'd got engaged? Are you pregnant?" Cheryl demanded.

"Hang on a minute, Cheryl. I'm just as shocked as you," I replied. "I had no idea about any of this. What am I going to do?" I asked.

Cheryl said, "Well that's a bit creepy." and I replied feeling a little hysterical

"Ha! Ya think!!"

On the drive home, I tried to talk to Matt about it, but he seemed so happy, it was weird. I did end up talking to Matt, but he said, "Why don't we just give it a try. Give it a couple of months then, if you still don't feel as if we could have a good life together, a family and everything, I will walk away."

He seemed so reasonable, so I felt it better just to agree. The thing was everyone really liked him: my friends and my family. He was a very charming man, most of the time. The months rolled on. The only things that made sense to me was that ever since he had mentioned having babies, my body clock had started ticking louder than ever. Maybe we *were* supposed to have a family together. This thought got into my head and wouldn't go away. Matt moved in on April Fools' Day (clearly I still wasn't listening to my intuition!).

I accepted a new position at work, which included longer hours. Matt began picking me up from the station, as I worked in the city and didn't get home till 6:00pm. He also had dinner ready for when we got home. So far, he had only given me reasons why I should marry him and I felt happy most of the time I was with him. Sure, we had the odd fight. Most people did, but we seemed to be heading in a good direction and the earlier hesitation I had felt started evaporating. We began talking about our future and planning for a wedding and children. Things started to move swiftly and then I found out I was pregnant.

A couple of months before the wedding, Matt and I went out for our usual weekly dinner date at a Vietnamese restaurant just five minutes drive from our home. It was comfortable and a good way to relax and catch up after a long day at work. We were sitting at the table we always sat at, which was close to the kitchen, as we enjoyed being able to talk to the staff more. Some of them were Matt's friends.

This particular night, the place was busy and the staff moved back and forth quickly. It felt more intimate and private sitting there without the regular catch-ups with the staff, and it gave Matt and me a chance to talk about our wedding plans and other things we had not had the time for during the week. Matt said something that I didn't quite hear, so I asked, "What did you say?" He replied, "It doesn't matter." Confused I asked him what he had said; again and again he replied that it didn't matter.

I was in a playful mood and said, "Come on, what did you say?" teasingly, but harmlessly. All of a sudden, Matt's whole face changed. I didn't recognise him – his face became so distorted. His eyes turned black and were devoid of soul. I was shocked at his transformation and as I was looking at him I heard a deep malevolent-sounding voice coming from him, saying "NOOOOOO!!!" It was the most terrifying voice I had ever heard in my life, and the look in his eyes told me that at that moment he wanted to kill me. I was terrified and didn't understand what was happening.

I looked at his body, but it wasn't him. Even writing this now, it is just so hard to put it on paper, because I know how crazy it sounds; it was truly terrifying. This face, the voice, the eyes – they weren't Matt's. I only knew that I was scared out of my wits by what I was seeing.

I didn't know who or what was sitting across from me. I started to lean away from him, but then his face changed yet again, and another voice – this time a softer English-accented, male voice came from him. It said, "I will not hurt thee. I will never hurt thee. Do not be afraid." The next moment Matt's face changed back to his own, and I could recognise him again.

I jumped up out of my chair and said, "What just happened, Matt? What the hell was that?"

"Never mind Karen, let's just get out of here!"

He got up, and went and paid the bill. Taking my hand, he tried to pull me out the back way through the kitchen.

I snatched my hand back and said, "I'm not going anywhere with you. Who the hell are you?"

"I'm me Karen," he replied. "You know it's me." He took my hand again and walked me outside. I didn't know what to think or do. I got into the car and sat petrified, pressed up against the door on the drive back to my unit – my mind was spinning. When he pulled up at home, I jumped out of the car. He got out of the car and started walking towards me. I stared at him shocked at what I'd seen.

"NO! Don't you come near me!" I cried. "You *have* to tell me what happened. I'm not going in there with you until you tell me."

So, there outside the flat, he began telling me a story of when he was in his late teens and he used to play in cemeteries with his friends. He said he believed that something or someone had attached itself to him during that time. I later found out that he had also used drugs. I discovered even later on that they can leave holes open in your aura, where beings that are lost and haven't gone over to the other side can sometimes attach themselves. It sounds mad doesn't it?

Trust me, I know how crazy this sounds. If I hadn't live through it myself, I'd think it was ridiculous, too. But, I can tell – hand on heart – it happened, and I had never been so frightened. I tried to get more information out of him, so I could understand what he felt when this had happened.

Where did he go while it was happening? Was he scared, too? But, he closed up and I knew that I couldn't press him any further, for now. In any case, I didn't want to in case that thing came back.

That experience was the catalyst for questioning, searching, and researching more about the psychic world. The weird thing is I could actually feel that what Matt had told me was real for him. I could also feel that whatever, whoever, it was had been there, in that moment, and that now, as he spoke to me, it wasn't. It had gone. Sleep didn't come easily that night and it was a very unnerving experience. I hoped I'd never see that ever again! However, that wasn't to be the case – Matt would have three more '*incidents*' over the next three weeks.

I was really unsettled by it and sought out a beautiful, spiritual, Aboriginal woman called Mona about whom I had been told. I called her and made an appointment to see her at her first available appointment, the following Tuesday at 05:00pm.

Things with Matt and I had returned to normal and I had begun relaxing again when he was around. That Sunday morning we were lying in bed. I had my head on his shoulder, but it was turned away from him. We were talking about what we would do that day and the week ahead.

I said, "I've made an appointment with Mona on Tuesday."

"Who's Mona?" he asked.

"It doesn't really matter, now, but I was so scared the other night. She's a psychic and I just wanted to talk to her about what happened with you, that's all." I felt something change in Matt. His body felt odd and cold and then I heard that voice, dripping with same evil tone,

"Oh where does she live?" it asked.

I froze. I could feel danger in every single word it uttered. I jumped out of bed and stood looking at Matt, who wasn't Matt at all, even with the small distance between us. I couldn't stop shaking. Then a second or two later Matt was back again, saying, "It's gone. I promise, Karen, it's gone."

I knew what he was saying was true. I could feel it, but I was still scared and crying, now.

"What the hell is that?" I asked myself more than anything. Matt tried to come near me, but I couldn't bear for him to touch me. "How do I know that thing isn't coming back? It hates me Matt. It wants me dead. I can feel it. What am I supposed to do, now?"

The days passed and I went to see Mona, although I never spoke of her again to Matt and he didn't bring it up either. I was hopeful she could shed some clarity and – hopefully – could help me understand whatever this was. I felt a little relieved that I was able to discuss it with someone else.

Sitting with Mona, I told her what had happened – everything that happened.

"I can't help you," she said.

I sat stunned by her words. "What am I supposed to do? We're going to be married soon."

Mona said simply, "Get out. Get out before you can't."

I was bewildered. The whole situation became even more unsettling, after I pressed her for any kind of help. She told me that she would try to contact someone, whom she thought might be able to help me.

"If they *can* help you they will call you. Here, take your money and go."

Upset, I left. Then I waited and waited, but no call ever came.

Two weeks passed with no 'intrusions' and things seemed fine. Then the following weekend, on our way to Cheryl's daughter's birthday party, we needed to stop at a 7-Eleven to pick up some snacks to take. Matt was driving, and as he turned into the street near the 7-Eleven the radio began crackling. I tried to fix the station, but the crackling persisted so I turned it off. The crackling kept on going. An icy-cold shiver went right through me. I turned to look at Matt and saw he was grabbing the steering wheel and his knuckles were white.

All of a sudden, he sped up, and then pulled into a parking space at the 7-Eleven petrol station, and turned off the car. He was frozen, staring straight ahead, with both hands gripping the wheel again. I was too petrified to move or speak. After a while, his hands dropped to his lap and his body relaxed.

I said. "It was back again, wasn't it?"

"Yes..." he replied... but, I wouldn't let it hurt you. All I can tell you is that it has gone for good this time."

He tried to explain it to me. He said he felt as if the top of his head had been lifted off and a lot of cold air just flew out of his head. Then it was gone. He said he was somehow sure that it was never going to come back. He seemed so shaken I believed what he said, and I could tell he believed it too. Feeling jittery from the whole experience, we headed into the 7-Eleven to get what we needed.

I went down to the back of the shop to get some drinks and things. When I got back to the front, I couldn't see Matt. I called out to him.

"I'm down here, Karen, near the DVD's." It wasn't Matt's voice. I went up to the front of the shop and saw Matt crouched on the ground. He turned to look at me sideways, and it wasn't Matt. That thing was looking at me with its evil face, smiling. I flew up to the counter and paid for my things, before rushing out to the car. By the time I got to it, Matt was already there, and it was Matt again, not that thing.

I said to him "Do you even know what happened in there Matt? I can't live like this anymore, I can't. I'm going crazy. This kind of thing doesn't happen in my world, it just doesn't. What am I supposed to do, now? You can't stay. I can't be with you, never knowing who you really are, and whom I'm going to be talking to."

"I wish I didn't love you. It would make things so much easier," I finished.

"Karen I –"

"Yes! I know Matt. It's not here. I can feel it too, now. I know when it is and when it isn't. Just let me drive, Matt. I can't think about this anymore. I feel sick. You won't talk to me about how it affects you when it happens, so let's just go to this birthday party."

I really needed to be around people right now. Ha! Safety in numbers and all that, what a joke. I wasn't laughing and neither was Matt. By the time we got to the party, I just wanted a drink and Matt kept his distance from me. I tried to feel normal, but I couldn't remember what that was actually like anymore. By the time we got home, we were both exhausted. I had a shower and got into bed, as did Matt. Tomorrow was Monday, so we both needed to be up early.

We eased ourselves back into 'normal' life: work, home, time for each other and it never happened again, at least not with that thing, whatever it was. I don't think Matt even knew. But whatever it was, it was gone. I knew it was gone. I didn't need Matt to tell me. My intuition had been put through some horrible tests, but it was working. Oh yes I absolutely knew it was working.

Life got back on track and we both tried hard to move on, and to move forward. Matt picked me up from the station after work and made dinner for us. We talked about our work days. Things appeared normal on the surface. We were both trying hard and we never went to that Vietnamese restaurant again. I had invested too much of myself in our relationship. I didn't want to give up on him, on us, so weeks drifted on and we found happiness in the simple things we enjoyed in our life together.

We were sitting in the sun in the lounge room, one Sunday afternoon, talking. He was in the chair and I loved sitting on the floor, so I rested my arm over his knee as we talked. We were talking about the wedding and that things were all organised and ready to go.

"Matt all we need is a celebrant now and Dad said he knows one who is a friend of his and he has agreed to marry us if we want. Matt, are you listening, Matt?" He felt strange, not scary strange, but different.

I turned and he looked peaceful, and felt peaceful, but I knew something was happening.

"Tell me what is happening to you. I can feel something, Matt, but I'm not scared"'

He told me he could see all these sparkles in a golden light as if they were raining down on him and it was a good feeling. It made him feel happy and relaxed. I believe someone came down to protect him, and to take that *thing* away.

Two years later the movie Ghost (1990) came out, and as soon as I saw it I remembered what Matt had told me about the light and the sparkles. It looked exactly the same as those in the movie.

*****

The thing about intuition and not following it is we always have a reason that seems to be justified at the time and there are lots of them. We are wrapped up in love, or the idea of love, and don't want to listen to anything that could destroy what we think we have.

Being pregnant is a big one. As women, the nesting gene takes over and making a family is all we care about, regardless of what may be going on in the world around us. There are so many reasons, take your pick.

Whatever it is, it is always more important to you than listening to the intuition knocking inside your head. Because, if we did listen to it we would have to act on it and sometimes not acting on it feels more important.

My circumstances were that we were having a baby. The day we got married in the park was the most beautiful day of my life. All I had thoughts for were our child and the home I was creating for our family. As far as the other '*thing*', I had buried any thoughts of that deep down in a place where even I couldn't find them. Now, was the time for some happiness and we *were* happy, very happy, for a few years.

It was only in hindsight (again hindsight is a wonderful thing) that I realised that I had been shown a glimpse of my life, if I married Matt. It occurred when my sister reminded me of those two movies we had seen years ago. The theme in both those movies ended up coming true for me, and the *crumbling house* was a great metaphor for our marriage, when I look back. Although our house didn't literally crumble, our marriage disintegrated and we both had to pick up the pieces from the ruins around us and find a way to move forward.

This is the way it is, sometimes, when we go against our deeper instincts and ignore our intuition. I needed to learn many lessons on my way to becoming the person I am today: lessons about my self-worth, not just as a woman and a mother but also as a human being. I learned what I was and am prepared to do and what I'm not. By ignoring what my intuition was telling me, I chose the hardest path. The road I was on was leading to one of those dark holes I spoke of earlier. I was tested mentally, emotionally and psychically on a level I never even knew existed.

Trusting what you know and feel inside yourself, and understanding the reasons why sometimes you don't (even though we know or feel on a deeper level that we should) are things that we need to address. Although, when we're doing what we've chosen to do, is probably not the time to learn this, unless you're in a position to do so. However, when you eventually do, or when I did, it is like a debriefing. Ensure you're in a safe place, and get out all your thoughts. Some will make sense and some won't.

I can come up with reasons why I married Matt and stayed with him for so long. We were making a life together and raising our family. We had a good start and I loved him. We were having a child together and having a child binds you. I also think that at the age of 35, I wanted to believe in the dream we're given as young girls, the happy ever after one. Even though I know that is a myth. But, I loved him, and I hope...

" Speak to me with words of wisdom and love.
For they move me,
as does the beauty of a single delicate flower
in a bed of thorns.
Create a special place in this world,
where love will blossom into the magnificent;
a special place where love is all.
Make it not a rarity in this world,
but live in a world where pain and loneliness
are driven into extinction!"

Karen N Sawyer 2000

CHAPTER 4

Dad and how his Passing Helped Me

I was in my late 30s when we found out Dad had lung cancer. He had had various other medical problems before his lung cancer, and had not aged well. He ended up having half a lung removed. He was told that he was clear of the cancer, which I thought was odd, as it had only been three months since his operation.

However, Dad was so happy to hear the news that I let it go. I ignored what I *felt*. I kept travelling up to the Gold Coast to see him each month or so, to look after his financial affairs, and pay his bills etc. I spent what time I could with him. A few days once a month seemed so little.

It was after one of these visits that I went to see another psychic, back home in Sydney. I felt something was really wrong with Dad; more that the state of his general health and dementia and I wondered if seeing a psychic might allay my fears? I know what you're thinking; why not speak to his doctors? That is a good question. The thing is his doctors were evading our questions, no matter how hard we pressed for any information. Yes, this kind of thing really does happen, or it did twenty-five years ago. Seeing a psychic was something I felt compelled to do... was it intuition? You tell me.

I looked in the local paper, feeling ridiculous, but safe in the knowledge that I would not have to explain my reasoning for doing so to anyone, especially not to my sister, who lived on the Gold Coast about twenty minutes away from Dad. She saw Dad as much as she could, but with two children under two, her hands were full at the best of times. I called the number of a psychic called Kitt in Kogarah Bay She lived about ten minutes drive from me. We made an appointment for the next day and agreed on the price.

The next morning I knocked on her door at the appointed time. I don't really know what I was expecting but Kitt wasn't it. She was very tall with crazy, long, blonde hair. She was so, so skinny, which was accentuated by her tight black jeans, equally tight black top and stiletto boots.

"Oh my gosh!" I thought, "I'm getting a reading from a chain-smoking witch!" She invited me in and as she led the way through a small lounge room to some stairs, I noticed a long shelf on one of the walls in the room. There were lots of crystals on it and a couple of candles. One of the smaller stones was a purple one that looked a bit like a pyramid and it caught my eye.

Kitt made her way up to a small room at the top of the stairs, as I struggled to get my son up in his stroller. I wondered if I was really meant to be here. However, once we got into the room I felt myself starting to relax as she spoke to me and explained how she did what she was going to do. Although I was trying to listen, my mind was focused on the cigarette hanging out of her month and the ashtray on her desk.

"Kitt, would you mind opening the window?" I asked pointing at my son in his stroller.

"Yeah sure" she said, "no problem."

She didn't stop smoking throughout the entire time I was there, but at least the smoke from her cigarettes went out of the window and not down into my son's lungs, or mine for that matter.

The reading she did was really interesting. Just before she finished I asked her about my dad.

"I don't do that kind of stuff," she said.

"I'm not asking you to tell me if or when he might die, Kitt. My dad lives in Queensland. All I'm asking you to do is to let me know if I should go up to see him more often. I just need to know, so I can have more time with him."

I could see her struggling with herself.

"Please Kitt; my husband hates me going to see my dad, because he doesn't like having to look after our children while I'm gone. It's not fair on my children either for me to be away so much. But, more than anything right now, I need to know so I can be there for dad as much as possible." I looked directly into her eyes, hoping she would change her mind.

Then she said, "I would make the most of the next five months if it was me."

I blessed her for her kindness to me that day. I also bought the purple amethyst crystal pyramid. I still have it, as the first crystal I ever bought. I learnt a valuable lesson that day. That is not to judge others by the way they look or the kind of clothes they wear. We all have a soul: the essence of who we're at the very centre of our being. Our soul does not need a look. Our soul does not need clothes. If you take the time to look into another's eyes and into its depths, you will see their soul and recognise your own. It is a space of no judgement, a space where fear cannot exist. It is the space of pure love.

Love is the only reality,
The reality of thy self
And therefore the reality of all

*****

Every time I went to see Dad we always went out for coffee. It was our thing and we spent these times catching up on what we'd both been doing. We'd get in the car and off we'd go.

"I've found a new café, Karen," he said.

I laughed, happy to be there and happy Dad was happy. My childhood had its moments of joy, but there were many troubles along the way and I feel safe speaking for both my brother and sister in this. The thing is the older I get the more mortal I feel. The only real gift I want is time, more time with those I love.

About five months after I'd been to see Kitt, we got a call from Dad's doctor. The cancer had come back and I couldn't help thinking, how utterly ironic, that I should have gone to – possible – the only chain-smoking psychic around. I laughed until I cried. Dad's surgery to remove the cancer in his lungs had not been successful.

The cancer has metastasised to his brain. We all knew what that meant. Dad decided against chemotherapy, opting for radiation therapy only. Because he was a war veteran, he was looked after very well, including having a taxi to pick him up and bring him home from these appointments.

I went up, the first time he went for his treatment, as I wanted to be there. I wanted to surprise him. I waited until the taxi had pulled up, and then I walked up his driveway to greet him. I was shocked at how quickly his physical appearance had changed, since my last visit only four weeks ago. What little hair Dad had had been shaved off and there were coloured permanent marker lines over his head that divided it into sections. Later he told me that they used these to do the radiation treatment.

The next morning, Dad wanted to go for a coffee.

"Come on let's go." He took his car keys and started walking to the door. He looked so frail after his treatment that I thought he shouldn't be going anywhere. I didn't know whether he was making this huge effort for me, or himself, or maybe for both of us.

"Okay Dad, I'm coming, but how about I drive this time?"

He stopped and waited for me, locked the front door, and handed me his keys.

"How about we go to that little cafe we went to last time? It's not too far and we both loved it. Remember Dad?" I suggested.

"I can't remember my own name half the time. Let's go then." He replied.

I grabbed Dad's favourite straw hat from the rear shelf in his car and gave it to him, and then off we went. Something happened while we were at the cafe, Dad sipping his cappuccino and me my hot chocolate.

It felt as if time stopped. There were people around, but everything outside Dad and I seemed to be in slow motion. It not only felt strange but eerie. There was only one thing I wanted to say, well ask really. We had all accepted what was happening to Dad and I felt that the time for pretence had passed.

"Dad, what do you believe happens when you die?" I asked.

He looked at me for a while and then said, "Karen, I don't know what happens once you die, but I'll tell you this. If there IS any way you could come back, then I will come back to you and let you know."

Tears filled my eyes and I could see them forming in his so I did what I always did and said, "You're not going to come back and haunt me are you?" We both started laughing and the moment was gone.

My visit was too short. About a week passed and then my sister called.

"Dad fell down his driveway, after he came home from his treatment today. Luckily the taxi driver was still there and helped him."

"Where is he now?" I asked. "Did he injure himself badly?"

"I don't know any details," she said. "I've left the boys with their dad and I'm heading over to the hospital now, Sis. I'll call you once I know what's going to happen."

She found out that Dad had to be hospitalised and this would be his home until, well... until. In one way, it was good, because it was much closer to my sister and she was able to take her boys to visit him. I stayed with her every time I went up after this.

Time slipped away, and Dad's health became worse. He was moved into the Code Blue Unit. The nurse told us that patients are transferred there, when they only have about six months left.

My final visit to see my dad came all too quickly, even although I didn't know it at the time. He was in and out of consciousness now and only recognised us for a few minutes at a time. I had been with him for three days and on the Saturday night, he said, "Look Karen, look whose here!" as I walked into his room. I could see no one.

"Who Dad, who is it, whose here?"

"Roy Tiker," he said. Roy Tiker was a long-time friend of Dad's who'd died a few years earlier. I remembered hearing somewhere that when a person is ready to pass over – to die – people they knew who are on the other side will come to them to help make their transition a little easier.

Dad's mentioning his old friend made me suspect that Dad was coming close to the end of his time with us. I guessed we had a few weeks, maybe a little more; no one can say with any certainty how long it takes it is different for all of us. I was staying positive and the next day, was Sunday, and I went to visit him before I flew home the following morning. I told him I would be back in a couple of weeks. My visit ended with a cuddle and a kiss for him, but mainly for me.

On Monday morning, I was getting ready for my sister to take me to the airport. I was nearly ready, and then something came over me, an incredible sense of panic. I could hardly breathe.

I yelled out to my sister, "I have to go to the hospital, now!"

"Karen we need to leave for the airport in half an hour," she said.

"I'll be back in time. I just have to go and see Dad, right now," I said as I ran out the door to get into Dad's car. My hands were shaking, as I drove. I got there and flew out the car and down the path to Dad's room. I stopped at the door and took a deep breath. Although I was still shaking I tried to look calm. Dad seemed to be sleeping.

"Hi Dad, are you awake?" I asked. He turned and looked at me. "Karen, my feet are cold."

"No worries, Dad." I took some socks out of a drawer and put them on him.

He seemed to doze off again and then he sat up and said, "Karen, are you here?"

"Yes, Dad I'm right here." He looked at me, into my eyes and I knew he was here in this room with me. "Karen, I've lived a good life. I've had a family I loved, and I've lived to see my children marry and become adults I'm proud to know. I've lived long enough to see my grandchildren born, but now I want to see my grandchildren's children born. It's not enough, this life we're given."

I hugged him tightly. We both knew, in this moment, that this would be the last time we saw each other, at least in this life. There was nothing left for us to say, only feel. The minutes had flown by and I knew I had to go, even though every part of me didn't want to. I pulled away. What do you say to a person when nothing is left unsaid? I kissed him on the cheek one last time and, with the brightest smile I could muster, I said, "Catch you next time Dad. I love you."

"I love you too, Karen."

I saw a light go out in his eyes and realised he had disappeared back behind his dementia. I left him and walked back up the path towards the car. I stopped and turned around one last time. I needed something, just something, to take with me and there he was sitting at his window with the biggest smile on his face. I smiled back waving, with tears falling. It didn't matter now. He couldn't see them.

As I watched him smiling up at me, a beam of morning sunlight hit the Golden Palm outside his window and the whole palm shone like gold beside him. That was the picture I took with me in my heart, as I turned and got into his car. I only drove thirty meters or so down the street – enough to be out of sight – before I stopped the car. My tears fell and I cried as though I would never stop.

Somewhere in the midst of all my pain I knew I had a plane to catch. I blew my nose and sniffed the tears away. I needed something to distract me on the way back to my sister's house. I turned the radio on. Elton John was singing 'Circle of Life." Blinded by my pain, this song only added to it and I cried even harder. It was not quite what I was hoping for, but it was probably the most appropriate song and it brings me to tears to my eyes every time I hear it and always will.

I never really thought of these things: the sun hitting the palm in exactly the right moment, Dad coming back to smile for me one last time or the song on the radio, as signs, but now I think how could they not have been? Something, or someone, was trying to show me that life does go on. On some level it goes on.

Three weeks later, my sister called.

"Karen, Dad passed away half an hour ago. Karen, are you alright?"

"No, but I'll be okay. I'll call you tomorrow, Sis. I love you."

"I love you too," she said.

I hung up the phone, slid down the kitchen cupboard, and sat rocking and holding my knees knowing I would never see my father again.

CHAPTER 5

Angels and Intuition

Dad's service was organised for the Friday after he passed, so that it gave people a chance to get there.

It was time and we all headed to the crematorium. My brother, his wife and my sister stayed outside speaking to some family as they arrived.

I touched my brother's arm and said, "I'm going to go in."

I walked inside and started walking down towards our seats. I saw Dad's coffin. I wasn't prepared, and imagined him lying in there. I turned and ran out. My brother caught me and hugged me. We took our seats, as the chapel filled up with relatives and friends, and the service began. I was there but not there, sitting in my own space and trying to hold myself together. As the service progressed, someone was asked to read a poem. I looked up ready to listen.

"*Go placidly amid the noise and the haste and remember what peace there may be in silence. As far as possible, without surrender, be on good terms with all persons...*"

Max Ehrmann (*The Desiderata*)

This poem held such significance for my father and me. It was on a card that he gave me when I was younger and these words have helped me so much in my life. Anything but this poem, I though! Try as hard as I might to hold them back, tears fell and would not stop.

My brother put his arm around me "You'll be okay," he said and he hugged me.

I whispered, "Dad gave me a card with this on it a long time ago. I can't –" I knew I was supposed to hold it together. That's what people do at funerals, but my tears kept falling and I didn't really hear anything after that. I was just sitting in my sadness and tears, hiding my head behind my hair.

"Weird!" I thought. I always tended to grown my hair longer, every time I didn't want people around me. Looking back, from here, I see now how that became one of the patterns in my life. Conversely, I'd chop it all off when I felt happy in myself, or was embarking on a fresh road, so to speak. I'm pretty sure you know what I mean.

I started to feel something warm. It felt as if a warm shower was passing right through my body. I looked up and, as I did, I saw a mirage of water moving to the back of the chapel, towards the heavy velvet drapes right behind the head of dad's coffin.

I sat and watched as those drapes started flapping around. Then I realised what was happening and laughter began to rise inside of me and bubbled its way up. I got a fit of the giggles.

I knew with absolute certainty that Dad was making good on his promise and that this was him letting me know he was still around. It was just like him, too. He had the 'gift of the gab'; everyone who knew him had said that all throughout our life. Dad just couldn't leave without having the last word, or in this case, making a last appearance. During the rest of his service and the day, I felt calmer and more in control of my emotions. Dad had let me know he was still around, somewhere, and that was enough for me to feel some comfort. Although my sadness was real and would be for a long, long time, that was enough and all I really needed at that time. Little did I know this was not the last time I would 'speak' with my dad.

One month later, and very early in the morning, we were all still in bed asleep. I woke up with a start and jumped upright. At first, I rubbed my eyes thinking I must still be asleep and dreaming, but no! It was still there on the other side of the room, where our mirrored wardrobe stood. There was – quite literally... doorway within a white light that was so brilliant. I'd never seen anything like it before. My dad was standing in the middle, looking so dapper in a black dinner suit and a white shirt, open at the neck. His right elbow was resting on the wall, although it didn't look like a wall, and his head was resting on his hand. His left hand was on his hip and his feet were sort of crossed at the ankles.

He looked much younger, like when he was in his 20s. I knew it was him because of an old photo we had that showed him when he'd just come back from WWII. That was way before I was even a thought in his mind. He reminded me of an old song he and mum used to sing when I was little, called 'Leaning on a Lamp Post'. It was as if he really was leaning on a lamp post. Anyway, the memories about this just came flooding back, I was really shocked at his being right here in my room. I just hoped he didn't wake Matt up!

Then Dad smiled at me. "What are you doing, Dad? Where ARE you?" I asked.

"I'm having a ball Karen. I'm having a ball. Don't be afraid, don't ever be afraid!" he replied.

In that moment, which seemed to last forever, he was smiling and young, not the old, sick man I had known as my father.

"Where are you? Where are you going?"

"You'll find out when it's your turn. There's nothing to be afraid of. I'm having a ball!" He smiled at me and then he just disappeared.

The light went out, and the *door* that didn't exist closed. Our room looked and felt as it normally did. The only thing that was different was me. I sat stunned for a minute. I realised we hadn't actually spoken our words – we had heard and answered each other's thoughts. I wasn't tired, so I got up and made a cup of tea.

Then, with my shaggy but cosy dressing gown on, I sat in the family room on the couch sipping tea and waiting for the morning noise to start. I tried to figure out what had just happened. I knew one thing for sure. It had happened and I wasn't feeling so sad anymore. I sat with my own thoughts, until my babies came to find me and another morning began.

Two weeks later, I had another dream. This one was similar, but different. I was standing in the main centre of one of our larger local shopping centres, called Eastgardens. The lower level was packed with people as it often is at holiday times.

People were rushing here and there, as if there was no tomorrow. I was standing in amongst the crowd, about forty feet away from the escalators. I was just looking around, when I caught sight of my dad coming towards me.

"Dad, Dad" I called out, but he didn't seem to hear me. He was heading to the escalators.

"DAD, I'm over here," I yelled. I waved my arms around, but he still didn't hear me. He also looked as he had during the last few months, before he died.

You know that feeling you get when you've been really looking forward to seeing someone for a long time and then you see them, but they don't see you or they don't know you're there. Then they turn a corner and you can't reach them and you feel a kind of sick emptiness inside you? Well, that's what I felt when I saw my dad step onto the escalator. I knew that, with all of the crowds, I would never get to him. All I could do was watch as he rode up the escalator.

I opened my eyes and realised I'd been crying. I was in bed and had been dreaming, but I knew, I had just seen and felt my father leave. He had gone – really gone – from this world into another. At least he was going up and not down...

My father's presence had helped me through my grieving process. I still grieve. None of us gets out of this, when there is love. Even now, a flicker of memory will pass across my mind and his loss still feels as deep. They say only time lessens the pain, but sometimes I find this isn't true, although the love and my memories can make me smile.

"Life is a journey defined by LOVE, in a moment or a lifetime."

It wasn't until much later that I realised my guardian angels were trying to show me that it was part of life, and that all was – and is – as it should be. But, when a child loses a parent or a parent loses a child, nothing can console or ease the enormity of the pain and the feelings of such a loss... nothing can. Nothing except faith, that is! Faith that this was part of his journey, as it was a part of mine. Faith that he is not in pain anymore. Faith that he is in a safer, happier place and is loved by all those who have gone before him. My faith in the goodness of all things is what keeps me moving forward, and keeps me going, especially in times like these. Part of my purpose is to keep looking for the goodness in things, the goodness in others and in myself.

"Look only for what you want to find and you shall find it."

*****

It was seven months since Dad had passed over. Things between Matt and I had not improved; in fact, they had gotten worse. I was lost, totally lost! I was so confused and couldn't think straight. Somehow, though, my intuition burrowed its way through and I began to breathe again and to listen and see the signs, guiding me on what I was to do. Once that began, I saw that everything was practically screaming at me to *go, and go NOW!*

Even when you know you should do something, sometimes the actual doing of it feels much harder than the comfortable cross you are already carrying. I had tried so hard to keep our family together, but I had been doing it out of fear, not love. For a long while, I'd tried to convince myself that everything would be okay, and I was getting through day-by-day. My main priority was making sure our children were as safe and happy as they could be. But, the minute I heard Matt's truck in the driveway, fear clenched my stomach as I waited, never knowing '*who*' would be walking through the door.

There had been a couple of times, recently, but nothing I couldn't come back from. However, the shame of knowing the children had witnessed them moved me to act, before anything else happened. The thought of how to get away was so loud it kept me awake at night.

I hadn't told anyone about my situation; not family, not friends, no one. I was terrified. I didn't want to wait until it was too late, but on the other hand leaving was something I hadn't wanted to do unless I could see no other choice and now, now he had left me with no other choice. I just needed some kind of confirmation, some kind of sign that my decision to leave was the right choice for all of us, and that the children would be safe in the process.

I went to see my psychic friend, Winnie. Maybe she could give me some clarity, as my emotions were all over the place. Winnie welcomed me into her home, and we sat in her office. Like me, Winnie records her sessions. She turned on the tape recorder and we began.

"You will be leaving, Karen. It will not be for a while yet, maybe the second half of the year. But, when the time comes you will not feel afraid. It will just happen, and he will know you are serious. Instead of getting angry, there will be a space of time where you won't have to deal with it, with him. I can feel how empty you are."

Tears started to come as acknowledgement of what I knew and felt to be true, although I was not ready to admit it.

"I promise you there will be a time around the end of the year when you and the children will feel happiness. Just know this is meant to be, and you will learn just how much strength you do have."

The past half hour with her had uncovered some really heavy stuff – even though, I knew deep down inside there was no other way... had to leave. Winnie led the way and we made a cuppa and sat down for a chat after which I felt lighter – still fearful of the future – but lighter.

So, our lives went on, and yes there was still fear, but there were also some happy times as a family and the time passed. In August, things took a turn for the best and the worst. Let me explain.

Matt and I had decided he should to go to a trade show in Queensland. I got all of the brochures and stationery he would need, while he was up there. I booked the flights and accommodation and everything was ready. It was Saturday night, and Matt was to leave the next afternoon. The kids and I were taking him out to the airport.

I was still angry over what I'd found yesterday, in the playroom we'd made for the kids, alongside the garage. I had gone in to get something I needed, which I saw up against the back wall. I moved carefully through all of the junk Matt had collected. Retrieving it, I turned and made my way back towards the door. That was when I saw what looked like some grass, behind a glass door in an old video unit we were throwing out.

I opened the cupboard and it was grass alright, but not the kind I was thinking about. It looked like a huge amount to me. I went inside, furious with him and the fact that he had lied to me again, and had put all our lives in danger. I called someone I knew could help me, and told them what I had found. They told me it was way too much to be considered for personal use and I had better tell Matt to get rid of it ASAP! This only deepened my resolve to end our marriage.

Sunday came around. I never thought I could make it till then, but I had to. The anger I felt towards Matt was eating away at me and I hadn't been able to sleep well for the past two nights. I felt as if I had been awake for ages. I looked over at Matt, who was sleeping. I watched him for a while, different emotions going through me and he woke up a few minutes later.

Then the words just came out of me in a calm voice that didn't sound like mine. "I can't do this anymore."

"Huh, what?" He was still half asleep.

"I said I can't do this anymore, Matt?"

"Do what anymore?"

"This, us, I can't do us anymore."

He was really awake, now.

"What do you mean Karen? Why? What's wrong, has something happened?"

"Apart from the 'normal' you mean? I went out to the kid's so-called playroom, which is still full of all your junk and I found it, Matt. I found it!"

I could tell by the look on his face he knew exactly what I had found.

"What were you thinking? What was going through your head the other night, when I was telling you I heard a house in our street – in the next block – was raided by the police and they found a huge lot of drugs on the premises! What do you think would have happened, if they'd have come here?"

I could almost see him thinking. "You could have told them you didn't know anything about it."

"Matt, I could have been taken to jail, and the kids would have been collected by Children's Services."

****

Thankfully, the airport was not too far from where we lived. Once there Matt and I got out. I stood by, as he said goodbye to the children.

When it came to me, I just said, "I think the space will help us to figure out where we need to go from here."

He was near to tears, but my heart was numb. "Will you pick me up from the airport next week?" he asked.

"Yes. Goodbye, Matt. We'll be here to pick you up."

The following Sunday his flight arrived. As he came towards us, the kids asked if they could play at the park for a while. After we put his things in the car and headed off, we stopped at the park and bought them an ice cream each. They played while Matt tried to convince me that everything was all okay. I was still in zombie mode. Eventually the kids came back and we all got in the car and headed home.

Matt even suggested we see a marriage counsellor. I agreed and the next day made an appointment with one for two days time. My fears were still real. I needed the safe space with the counsellor to get Matt to understand that our marriage was over. Nothing could bring back my feelings for him, and I asked him to move out.

Do I regret it, marrying Matt? Yes and no. What I don't regret is the time love was with us. For that small fragment of time, I felt loved and there was nowhere else I would rather be and no one else I would rather be with. I was totally content and fulfilled by the knowledge of that and the feeling that came with it. Especially, with the two most amazing children that came from our love. The unconditional love I feel for them is the gift of my life.

I will never regret the lessons I learned or how I became a stronger woman and a more kind and compassionate human being. All the other things I learnt with Matt also pushed me further along my spiritual and psychic path. What I do regret is the pain; the physical and emotional damage he caused and the space that was left empty by our child that died, before he got the chance to live.

*****

Many years had passed since then and except for when the children, now adults, mentioned him in passing, I never really thought about Matt any longer. One early morning, about 7am, I was on my way over to Mum's to have Christmas breakfast with her, as was the custom we had developed over the years. I was heading along the main road; the shops on one side and the bay on the other. I never got tired of this view. As I stopped at the lights, waiting to turn right to go to Mum's I saw him: a tired, lonely figure standing in his boat, alongside the net, where we had first met. The tears and the love I thought had dried and died long ago spilt over as I watched him, silently from the safety of my car.

I cried for the love I'd lost along the way and for all of the broken dreams I'd left behind. I watched, as he stood sewing the broken strands of net together, like the broken threads of our marriage that could never be mended. I cried for myself, for the love lost and for the lonely embittered old man who stood in the boat alone in his world, with only the sea to support him. I cried, until – finally... was able to say goodbye.

The lights changed and I headed away from the beach, and away from the man, I had loved so long ago. Now, I finally allowed myself to feel the freedom to go and find my future...

"When trusting blindly is what you know,
but may not be what you need,
lessons are everywhere!"

CHAPTER 6

Possibilities

I had been separated for only two weeks, when Winnie called me.

"Hi Karen, I'm running a course on learning to trust your intuition. I thought you might like to come along. It will get you out of the house and it's only one night a week," she explained.

"Oh Winnie you're priceless." I laughed. "Where was this eight years ago? Yes, of course I will. I'll see if Mum can come and look after the kids. Send me the details and I'll be there. Thanks."

I sat for a moment thinking about how quickly the universe works when we choose a better path for ourselves. Just then, a memory popped into my head. It was the memory of that dark evil thing that came through Matt, all those years ago. However, there was no fear now, as I remembered the look in 'its' eyes, and the depth of hatred it felt for me.

Now, the most important thing I remembered was the way it looked at me. It looked as if it really knew who I was. Its look told me it knew me much more than I knew myself and that's what I think really frightened me. It made me want to know myself better than anyone else could, and this was exciting to me. Scary, but exciting. I couldn't wait to start the class with Winnie.

I wanted to push myself to search, to discover, and to learn more about myself and about my intuition. Until it became a natural part of me again, and not an extra piece that I used every now and then when I thought about it. Rather, the way I used to be, and the way I used to see the world through the spiritual self. So, Winnie's course and timing were perfect after all!

The course was so interesting and opened my mind to lots of possibilities. I found the classes exciting and loved every moment of them. I was learning and absorbing like a sponge, such was my thirst for knowledge. My abilities came back so quickly, with the consistency of the classes and I felt I was finally being given permission to explore and grow my psychic abilities.

I discovered something new and exciting in each class. Having failed at maths in school, I found it ironic that I also found a love for numerology during these classes. I mean I couldn't even balance a cheque book, for goodness sake. Now, I know a lot of younger people will not even know what I'm talking about, but let me say this. Just because you may not be good at something in school, don't think that you cannot become great at it later on. School is one small step on our journey of discovery and thirst for knowledge.

"Remember!
If you never give up,
you will succeed at anything
you put your mind to."

Winnie was so relaxed and a matter of fact about the spirit side. She instilled confidence in all of us and I allowed myself to open up in the safe and sacred space that she provided. I felt like a child discovering the joys of life all over again.

It also made me think about my children, and I wanted to encourage them to express their inner selves. By allowing them the safety of free expression, I hoped they would also feel freer to become more defined human beings; young people who were unafraid to express their uniqueness in front of others. Of course, this was naive on my part. They were still very young, although they have each forged their own lives, over the years. They are each unique in their own way and how they take on life and living.

There were twelve of us that first night and we were down to eight after two classes. Sometimes we might think we want to learn something, but the timing is not right, or you find it is not exactly what you're looking for. This happens all the time during our life, and that is normal. There is a saying, "When the pupil is ready, the teacher will arrive." I believe this. I only have to glance back through my life to know just how true this is.

During the classes, Winnie introduced us to different kinds of modalities, to use as sensory instruments to tap into our intuition. Different things worked for different people. What I mean by this is that some *tools* helped more than others did, for each of us. As I said before, numerology really grabbed my interest, but I might not feel I want to use it all the time. It depends on the person that I'm with, and what resonates more with them.

We were given crystals to hold, as well. At some point, a card was handed around for us all to look at and we were each asked to say what we *saw* in this card. I was the last one to look at it. Everyone else in the group had said things like "I saw a river with lots of people around it. It feels beautiful and peaceful." Most of the girls seemed to pick up on this, too. As soon as I touched that card, my whole body recoiled and I dropped it. I didn't want to say what I'd seen. It was too awful and so unlike what the others had seen that it looked out of place.

Winnie encouraged me to speak about what I had seen.

"There isn't a right or wrong answer. We all come from different lives have different experiences so we don't always see the same things or see things the same way," she said.

Eventually I told them. "I couldn't hold onto the card. All I could feel was death – death everywhere. It was smothering me. I couldn't breathe. It was only for a second, but I saw a dead person standing in the opening of the chapel doorway, and there were bodies everywhere and lots of blood."

I actually felt as if I wanted to throw up!

"You were right, you were all right" Winnie said. "Most of you picked up on the landscape outside the church grounds and the compound, whereas Karen saw what had happened inside. It is a picture of 'The Alamo' in America, where a huge massacre took place in their history."

Later in the course, this example cropped up again. Winnie was teaching us about psychometry: the reading of objects. Someone had a Hibiscus flower. The other girls were mainly looking at the relationship of the woman who had brought it. Loving and in the beautiful garden from where she told us the flower had come. It was my turn, and this time I was in the middle of the group. I looked at the flower and burst out laughing.

"What did you see Karen?" Winnie asked. "I still feel silly from the vision I saw" I said, but I went on to tell them. I saw a man sitting at a table with a red and white checked tablecloth. He was shovelling pasta into his mouth as quickly as he could and there was a half-full glass of red wine glass beside him." All of the girls laughed with me. That's when the owner of the flower told us that while most of the girls had picked up on the loving relationship of the woman and her husband, I had *seen* the Italian restaurant they owned. I never doubted myself after that. What more proof did I need? There were many other examples throughout the years.

*****

Past Lives: I am separating this memory from the course, and will explain why at the end of it.

It was the first meditation we did in Winnie's Workshop. She told us she was taking us back to a past life. After she had guided us through each step, she eventually has us stop in front of a small, curved, wooden bridge.

"What do you look like in this life? I want you to walk across that bridge. When you get to the other side, you will see something. What is it? Pick it up and hold it. This is your reason for being here: to remember."

I looked down at my body. It was that of a young girl of about fifteen years old, with beautiful brown skin. I could see that my hair was straight and black. As I stepped onto the bridge, I looked over into the water to get a better look at myself. I looked pretty, like all fifteen years old girls do, regardless of what they think, and my hair was cut in that Cleopatra style, so I guessed I must be somewhere in Egypt. I continued over the wooden bridge. On the other side I saw a small woven cradle. In it was a huge white feather.

It was then that Winnie brought us back. I was blown away and thought that none of it could have been real, yet I knew without a doubt that it was. I remembered that I'd had some dreams that had seemed so real and in fact, when looked at with supporting evidence, it actually helped me to make some sense of a couple of things in my life that I had struggled with over the years. But, that's enough of that.

Winnie asked me what I had seen. I told her and the group this.

"I saw the Cradle and the Feather."

"What does this mean to you Karen?" she asked.

"Justice for the Children!"

These words came without thought, and once spoken, I knew they were my truth. My life took on a whole new meaning. When consciously connected, I looked at what I was doing right now, for myself and my children and those words rang true in a deep place in my soul.

*"We are all children;
learning, pushing boundaries,
adapting and, then, overcoming…
We shed our chrysalis, to become our purpose."*

*****

Further on in this book I will mention déjà vu and how these moments translate for me in my life. Well, I'm actually having one of them at his very minute, as I type this part about past lives. When they present in my life, it is a sign for me that I'm on the right track. So yes, confirmation here, I'm exactly where I'm meant to be in this exact moment. In other words, I'm meant to be writing this, at exactly this time. No doubts here… nope!

Ha ha ha ha ha! I so looove what I do, and the fun that happens in it. And to think that this Past Life piece and the New York piece, which is in a chapter further along, only came back into my memory this morning. They actually came to me as I was thinking about the other things I had to complete to finish this book.

*****

The first thing I did after the course was over was to try to test myself with something simple.

Every now and then, the police would set up a radar just over a hill on the way home between Mum and my place, so that if you were doing over the speed limit at the top of the hill, it would be too late to slow down. The thing is you nearly always had to speed up a little to get over this hill, especially in my old car.

About a week later, the kids and I were on our way home and I had totally forgotten about the radar as you do. Just as I was putting my foot down on the accelerator, to get up the hill, my foot stopped and I thought 'that's weird'. Then, I remembered the radar and I deliberately slowed down, to see if my intuition had reminded me that the radar was there this day. As I got over the hill, imagine how excited I was to see the radar. Not a common occurrence I can assure you. Two things had happened: 1. My intuition had warned me. 2. I had taken notice of it. Yeah me! I was so happy and I continued to play games with my intuition, each time proving it was working.

*****

The more I used my intuition, but consciously this time, the more I realised I had been using it unconsciously throughout my whole life. Without even thinking about it, I came to understand its purpose in my life. It was a sense, just as real as breathing, and just like the other five senses that the majority of us use every day through our eyes, ears, nose, tongue, and skin.

Can we explain why the other senses become heightened, when a person loses a sense; say, for sight example? Could this perhaps be their intuitive sense automatically kicking in to help enhance the other senses? To maybe compensate for the one they lost? I'm not asking you to accept what I'm saying, just because I'm saying it. But, if you're reading this book, then I think we can agree you're interested to discover more about the psychic self. It can be a lot of fun during the process.

Dictionary.com gives the meaning of 'sixth sense' as: "a power of perception beyond the five senses; intuition: *His sixth sense warned him to be caution*" is the example given There are too many of these kinds of examples for any of us to ignore completely. Even in my own life, I've too many examples of intuition at work to ignore the '*signs*' that have guided me along this life path.

However, just because I *know* this to be true with all my heart it does not mean that I have, or always do listen to my intuition. Yes, even as a psychic, I can ignore it. I live in the same physical world and have the same physical life as you do. Our days can be filled with joy or sometimes filled with frustration. That means we can ignore, or not feel, the signs around us or the feelings we have about something important (or even the kind of cake our friend likes), for example. That's because sometimes it's a matter of just getting through the day. Sometimes things just happen that shake your confidence and then, we might question our own judgement or our own thoughts.

I had lost a lot of my confidence, and not just my intuition, over those eight years with Matt. I can remember just knowing I was always a good judge of character, for example, but certain choices I made, had me questioning everything about myself. After I began to heal, I began to realise I didn't need to question myself. Everything I *knew* was still here inside me. I had only forgotten how to find it. Now was my time to remind myself who I was, not who someone else told me I was. I found this to be not only exciting but also extremely empowering!

It was also exciting as I discovered I loved learning, even more than I did before. The more I began to learn, and to trust and consciously use my intuition again, the more I felt like my whole self. I started listening to what I truly felt, instead of being so full of fear that my intuition didn't have a chance to do its thing. I went back to the basics and it is in the basics of anything that we learn the rhythm. Everything in life has a natural rhythm, a natural flow to it. Once you master moving in that flow, it is where you eventually learn how to fly. For me, flying comes not just in the believing, but in the 'knowing and the responding' to it.

For instance, I hadn't really thought about the things I took for granted as being somehow connected or mixed in with my intuition. They were things that I just knew were part of me, such as the weather thing. I had had that ever since I was in my early twenties and had gone on a house-boat holiday for a week with some friends. It was the first week of December and we were booked to take out the Halverson Cruise boat on the Friday. My friends were all so worried about the weather. It had been raining, I mean huge thunderstorms, for a couple of weeks, and more were predicted in the weeks leading up to Christmas.

I said, "Don't worry. We're going to have perfect weather."

We met at Bobbin Head and made our way to the pickup point with all our stuff for the week ahead. It rained all the way on the taxi ride out. We were to board at 2:00pm. At 1:30pm the rain stopped and, apart from a few left over clouds, the sky was blue and sun shone.

It remained like this for the next seven days: cloudless blue skies, warm days filled with swimming, sunbaking, fishing, and BBQs. It was perfect. It was also my mum's birthday, when we got back to the jetty the following Friday.

We collected all our stuff and after a few phone calls, waited for the taxis to pick us up for the ride home. We were an hour late in returning to the dock and I was worried Mum would knock and I wouldn't be there. I was taking her out for dinner, so it was decided I would go in the first taxi. All of this went to plan for me. I met Mum and we had a wonderful dinner at the restaurant. After I returned home, I unpacked all my stuff. I found out later – on Saturday morning – that everyone else in the group weren't so lucky.

Apparently, their taxis were all delayed because of a huge thunderstorm that came up all of a sudden, about half-an-hour after I left. This thunderstorm didn't stop until Christmas. I laughed about it, although my friends didn't find it as funny as I did. Anyway, after the holiday was truly over and Mum and I had a good time celebrating her birthday, I stopped and thought about how weird – like crazy weird – it all was.

I kept doing what I had done then. Every time I was going on a holiday I asked, prayed, requested that the weather for my holiday be perfect, and – I'm not making this up – it actually has been perfect weather, whenever I've gone on holiday. This has been happening for so long that even my friends don't question it. Oh and perfect does not have to mean sunny every day.

One year, my girlfriend and I really wanted to see a movie that had just come out while we were away. However, it was so nice just swimming at the beach or lazing around the pool that we couldn't be bothered. At some point during this holiday, I said, "I really would like to go and see that movie." Funny thing was that the next day it was cloudy. Not swimming weather at all, so we got to see our movie at a morning session. We stopped to do some shopping and then grabbed something for lunch and walked back to the unit we were staying in. The sun came out about half-an-hour after we got back. My girlfriend just looked at me and shook her head. I started laughing. I know you think I'm making this up, but I promise you I'm not.

Now, I've mentioned that I don't believe in coincidences, and I want to tell you another story that eventually helped to prove to me that my father was indeed trying to contact me after he had passed away.

It happened long before my father ever became sick. A close friend of mine, Cheryl, whom I mentioned earlier, and her husband were going to the Aria Awards. They had a beautiful little daughter, who was about three at the time. I was over having a meal and they were talking about needing to find a sitter for the night. I had grown fond of their daughter and said, "I'll do it. I'll look after Lucy for you." Cheryl said, "Really, are you sure?"

"Of course" I said. "We'll be fine, so I'll be here on Saturday night." We arranged a time and after a cuppa I headed back home.

I turned up on Saturday and Lucy was already in bed and sound asleep. After Cheryl had told me a few things I might need to know, and what time they would be back, they left. I made a cup of tea and settled down in the lounge room.

I turned on the TV to watch a movie. It was an uneventful night, except for once, when I heard Lucy getting out of bed. I went to her bedroom door and waited for her to turn the handle. When she didn't turn it, I opened the door to find her sound asleep and tucked up in bed as Cheryl had left her.

"That's odd," I thought as I walked back to the lounge room and settled back to finish watching the movie. I wasn't aware of the time, but I was nearly finished watching my second movie, when I heard Cheryl and Tony arrive home.

"Wow! That went quick," I said. "How was it?"

"It was a really good night." Tony said, while Cheryl checked on Lucy who was still asleep.

"I'll make us a cuppa," she said and Cheryl headed towards the kitchen.

Tony came into the lounge room and settled in an armchair next to the lounge I was sitting on. Then, I felt it.

Tony looked at me straight away and said, "You felt her didn't you?"

"Was that her?"

He nodded.

"It felt amazing, like nothing I've ever felt before. It was like a soft warm shower except the water went straight through my body. I felt incredibly calm and peaceful and, I wasn't scared."

Tony said, "I know. She's amazing isn't she?"

I got up and went straight out to the kitchen.

"Oh my God, Cheryl I felt her, I felt the little girl who lives here," I said with a big smile on my face.

"Yes, I wondered why you offered to babysit." she said.

"Because, I totally forgot you told me about the ghost who lives here," I replied. "I definitely wouldn't have come, if I'd have remembered! I'm so glad I did now. It... she, felt amazing!"

My memory of this came back to me at my dad's funeral, and this was how I knew he was still around in some form. Would I've noticed what happened to me at dad's funeral, if I hadn't experienced the little girl years earlier? Who knows? But, I believe with everything in me that it happened so I would be aware.

So that my subconscious – my inner guidance system – would recognise the feeling as it went through me, as well as the calm and peace I felt, even with so much time in between.

For me this was no coincidence. It was my dad helping me in my grief.

"*Your subconscious self moves through life*
in comfort and peace,
being and responding as the whole self,
without fear of retribution.
It resides at the centre of the soul;
your soul,
the centre of self love."

CHAPTER 7

Avalon

It was time to put our house on the market. I saw a real estate agent and signed up. I was taking my children on a holiday to East Beach, one last week of peace before the house was sold, but I had to find us somewhere to live in the meantime. We were heading down the coast on Sunday. On Saturday night, my agent called to say he had one woman through that day who seemed quite interested.

I said, "That's great. We will be leaving in the morning and away until the following Saturday night, so you have free run for inspections whenever you need to. I'll give you a call after that weekend to touch base."

The kids were excited for our holiday, so getting them to sleep was hard, but eventually we all got there. I packed as much of the car as I could and headed for bed myself. In the morning, we had a quick breakfast, finished packing the car, and were on the road within an hour and a half. With two small children in tow, I thought I did pretty well. East Beach was the last time we all holidayed as a family, so for me it was bittersweet. But, children are so resilient and couldn't wait until we got there.

We all had such a fun time, even on one day when it poured with rain, as we got to explore some of the shops close by. But, all holidays come to an end. On the last day the kids were playing outside with some friends they had made during the week. I was sitting inside the cabin I'd rented for us (not really a tent kind of gal, unless of course it a glamour tent).

Anyway, I was feeling so, so sad, knowing that our home would be sold to the first person, that woman, who had looked at it before we left. I had thought I would have more time. I wanted more time, but life had other things in mind for me and for us.

On the drive down to the beach, I'd had a 'feeling'. I knew our home would be sold in three weeks. What was that feeling? How did I 'know'? It's hard to explain, and as I said, we all experience things differently. But, for me it started after the course, where I had learnt to trust in myself and the things I felt, heard, or saw in my mind's eye. But, I will go into that further later. What matters is where I was at this point in my life.

I was at a point where I was truly trusting myself. On the drive down to East Beach, I heard the words "*In three weeks it is sold. The first person who looked bought it.*" As these words were passing through my mind, I felt a knowing and I knew it was true! As I said, it begins with trusting yourself.

Part of me wished it would take longer, but as I've come to realise over the years, everything happens with perfect timing. When things happen in your life, either good or not-so-good, they happen when they are needed.

The good seem exciting at the time and I venture to say that most of you will think, wow I'm so lucky! Really though, it means that you've been making positive choices for yourself and the good things come because you're living in the flow of your purpose. The not-so-good things come to show you that you're taking a harder road than you need to. They come to make you – to make me – stop and think about what we want and why we think we don't deserve it. Because if whatever it is for you hasn't shown up in your life yet, you can be sure that your thinking is behind it.

I was sitting in the cabin feeling sad about returning home, and knowing I only had about nine weeks to find us a new home, pack up this one, and move. I still had no idea to where, I allowed myself to wallow for... about ten minutes, and then I knew I would feel better if I took some control. So, I did what I knew how to do. I played a game. This game would give me a place to start. I felt better already.

The game? A makeshift sort of a game that we played as children, by folding a piece of paper over and over after writing a word on each corner. You may remember what I'm talking about. That day I called it 'where am I going next?' I got a bowl, a piece of paper and a pen. I divided the paper up into eight pieces. I wrote a direction on each piece; north, north-east, east, south-east, south, south-west, west, north-west. Simple, but effective. You can guess what comes next. Scrunched up each piece, put them in the bowl, and swished them around.

I took a minute to stop, breathe, and centre myself, releasing all thoughts of worry, wishing, and fear. I then asked myself 'which direction am I moving in?' I reached into the bowl and pulled out a piece of paper. North-east! Okay, so further north and closer to the water than we lived now. That was in the Sutherland Shire, south of Sydney. I felt better, although it would take a lot of work on my part to determine the best new home for our little family.

That night, before bedtime, I put the TV on for the kids so they could watch their favourite show, while I went into my bedroom to meditate for ten minutes. I was sitting on the bottom of the bed about halfway through my meditation, when I came out of it with a start. I felt disorientated for a minute and then I moved up to the head of the bed. I had only just reached it when the door to my room crashed in and fell right across the bottom of my bed, right where I had been sitting.

The kids had been instrumental in the door's crashing down. I had told them that if they could sit quietly for ten minutes, I would put the TV on for them and give them an ice cream each. Of course, they agreed and, of course, as every mother knows, bribes mean nothing and don't stop children being children.

Ice creams finished and TV found to be boring, they decided to have a game of chase. One of them slammed into my sliding bedroom door, and it came straight off the track and crashed down onto the bottom of my bed. I could have been killed! The kids screamed! I screamed! Then, I realised just how lucky I was, or that someone really was looking after me. My kids were so upset no punishment I could have dealt out would be worse than what they were feeling and how sorry they were. After a long cuddle together, I got them into bed and then I did the same.

On the drive home the next day, I thought about what had happened on our little holiday. The kids had had a great time playing and making new friends. I had a direction to follow to find our new home and the door crashing down was the sign I needed to know moving was the only way to grow. It was a positive step in the right direction our lives were about to take. As I've said, everyone's 'signs' are different, but once you learn to trust what yours are, it can be really exciting for you – if it isn't already.

After we arrived back home, I unpacked, did washing etc. while the kids ate the takeaway I'd bought on the way home to save cooking. The rest of the day was easy. The next day, after dropping my children off at school and pre-school, I stopped into the agent's for an update. There had been a few people through during the week, but no offers yet. Two weeks later, the agent called to say the woman, who had looked at the house first, had put in an offer. I accepted and the process of selling and finding something else began.

The following weekend, the kids went to their father's. After dropping them both off at school and pre-school on Friday morning (my ex would be picking them up from there when school finished), I left to spend the weekend with a girlfriend who lived at Palm Beach.

Being in Palm Beach was like being in another world. I felt the energy change around me as soon as I entered this amazing place. The natural beauty, the beaches and the peace, seemed to permeate right through me. The weekend was just what I needed. Being able to step outside of my life gave me a better perspective of it, and I knew we would settle into our new home easily and life would become simple. Now, I just had to find it. Easier said than done, and as the weeks went by I began to get frustrated.

I had about three weeks left before the house settled, and I was starting to panic. I was on my way up to Palm Beach again for the weekend, while the kids were with their father. I had just come through the bends, as the locals called it, which led into Avalon and up to Palm Beach. I was going through Avalon shops and stopped to pick up some things to take to my girlfriend's place. The worry and the fear I was feeling, knowing I needed to come through for my children, was tormenting me.

After I had got back into the car, and before I continued on to Palm Beach, I sat and allowed the desperation I was feeling out.

"I need a sign?" I said aloud. "Please give me a sign. Where am I meant to go?"

Even voicing my fear out loud helped me to feel a bit calmer. I took a few deep breaths and knew something would show up. As I started the car, I put the radio on to help lighten the mood I was in. The first thing I heard was Bryan Ferry singing *"Avalon"*

WOW!!! Now that just blew my mind. Yes psychics can still be surprised about lots of things. Certainly about their own journey and especially when clients come back to tell me how what I'd told them had manifested; some not in the way I thought they would, but still exciting to know. I will go into this, later. Spirit has a sense of humour, at least that's what I've found. It would be rather dull if they didn't.

So now, I knew exactly where we were to go. I spent the weekend looking. Funnily enough, I ended up being drawn to two houses in Palm Beach that I really liked. I spoke to the agent who was handling both of them and organised a look through that afternoon, before I had to leave to go home. Both of them definitely met my brief. True, they were much farther north and closer to the water than our house.

The first house in Palm Beach, which I had decided against, had seemed perfect, until I ventured inside to have a look. It was perched high on Sunrise Road and sat directly between the beach to the east and the Pittwater to the west. The sun streamed in. It had a real fireplace in the living room, good-sized bedrooms, and a workable kitchen. I thought how wonderful it would be waking up there. That is until I went into the bathroom. It was a long old-looking bathroom and appeared very clean. The door opened to the right.

"The shower is behind the door" the agent said. I felt a freezing cold sensation go right through my body. I moved the door and as I pulled back the shower curtain, I stifled a scream! I turned quickly, desperate to get out of that room. Once outside, I started to calm down and told the agent I was ready to look at the other house, the one we eventually did move into.

What was in the shower? There was the naked body of a dead girl with long, dark hair. She was slumped over the side of the shower and there was blood everywhere. Of course, she wasn't really there, but what I saw was real enough. It was also the first time I had seen anything like that. I feel sick just thinking of it, even as I write, now.

This was spirit making sure I made the best decision for us by choosing the other house. It was a safe, light, bright house, where we saw the cloud rolling out from The Hawksberry River and making its way out to sea like fog. That house showed me the goddess of Palm Beach in all her glory, lying in the water at the endpoint of Palm Beach, under the lighthouse. It sat at the highest point in Palm Beach, in Bynya Road, and looked over the Pacific Ocean to the horizon. Life was happy and relaxed here in our beach house.

Within a week of moving in, a woman knocked at the door. She would later become a friend. That day, she asked, "Would it be okay if your son came over to play with my son? They go to school together and he is the first person my child has wanted to spend time with?" Things were moving quickly. They always do when you're in the flow of your best life.

The only blip occurred early one morning, when I felt that 'thing' in my room again. I woke to see 'it' crouched in the corner of my room; a horrible dark image with those same eyes that had looked at me out of Matt's. This time though, I felt no fear. I was only pissed off and I told it so. "Get the fuck out of my house and out of my life and never come back!!!" In a moment, there was nothing there, nothing to be afraid of and nothing to worry about anymore. I knew I would be fine, and the children would be fine. No, actually I KNEW we would all be amazing!!!"

P.S., a few years later, we ended up living in Avalon.

*****

It was a cold morning in the middle of winter and Avalon Beach was empty of its usual morning rush of surfers and '*old timers*', who swam all throughout the year. I actually became one – not an old timer – but someone who swam throughout the year. It became one of the joys of my life. Whatever the weather, I loved the beach.

Today I hadn't been down to swim. It wasn't a great day, and after the children had gone to school, I decided to go for a walk to clear my head. I ended up at the beach, anyway. I began walking along close to the water's edge with thoughts swirling in my head. I'd walked about half way when this deep feeling of tiredness came over me. I couldn't walk a step further, so I stopped and turned to look out at the water.

I felt lost. I had built a good life for us up here, and we had all made good friendships, but something was missing for me. I had lost hope. I felt as if my life had come to a complete stop. I had come so far and yet I still felt as if I had nothing to dream about, nothing to hope for and I had nothing to work towards.

The weight of these thoughts was too heavy for me to carry and I walked away from the water. I just plopped down on the sand in the middle of the beach and let my tears fall. It didn't matter, because was no one there to see.

I don't know how long I was sitting there, when a cold gust of wind swept around me and down under my legs, which I had pulled up against my chest and wrapped my arms around. It felt so odd that it forced me to look down, I saw a tiny piece of paper drop onto the sand right beside my left leg. How weird I thought, especially went I felt no other wind or breeze. Then, it just stopped.

I picked up the bit of paper and turned it over. It was quite literally about the size of a five-cent piece and burnt around the edges, no doubt courtesy of an overnight log fire on the beach. There was something written on it, so I moved it up closer so I could see... *wish*... one word in the middle. I just kept looking at it. I couldn't believe what I was seeing... *wish*... nothing else just... *wish*.

Tears came straight up and out. I was crying so hard
I didn't think I would stop. What could I do with a
wish, when I didn't know who I was anymore? When I
wasn't sure what I wanted anymore? When everything I
wanted turned out to be an illusion.

I was too scared to make a decision, and so scared of making a wrong decision that I told my angels "please make this for me. You know my heart better than I do, right now." I took my '*wish*' home with me, still too afraid to speak of it. I still have that tiny piece of paper to this day.

If I'm being completely honest with you, and with myself, in the deepest part of my heart I did know what my wish was, but I was too afraid to put a voice to it for fear of losing it. *It was all I had left of me...*

"Fear and self-doubt can cripple,
but the light of God shines from within,
warming even the coldest space.
When you least expect it,
a miracle arrives,
and you are home."

CHAPTER 8

Spiritual Conversations

When I really began wanting to learn more about my spiritual psychic side in earnest and how it could work in my life, if I embraced it to the fullest, I began by playing games I tested my thoughts against what was actually happening or true. This was after I had developed my intuitive side to such an extent that the small element of any doubt that I had had earlier had been completely wiped away.

It started with trusting my thoughts about radar set-ups, and about *'seeing'* a parking space in the shopping car park at the busiest times of year. I'm sure a lot of you have done this and its fun, unless it doesn't work, and there will usually be a reason for this. Maybe you're hoping: something, which has your emotion attached to it, instead of trusting that it will be there for you, and then completely letting go of the outcome. The emotion comes when you're in your parking space.

When I enter a parking area or even just before, I ask "Please show me the perfect parking space for me today." Then I sit back and go with the flow, because I find that if I rush in actively looking for one I'd never get it. Once I relax and trust it will be there, wherever there is, then sure enough it will be waiting for me, just as I knew it would be.

Most of the time, I could drive in and a spot was available straight away. Sometimes, I would get a feeling to drive in another way and to another section. Other times, a car would put its engine on, just as I was approaching it.

For me that meant listening to the subtle signs, as I was driving, and trusting that my spot will be there, all the while. Sometimes, it was much further away than I would have liked, but when I thought about it; I hadn't been for a walk that day, so this was a way of getting me to do the walk anyway.

If a car tried pushing in front of me, I let it. If a car in front stopped longer than it should I never got anxious, because I had learnt to stop resisting. STOP RESISTING! Life flows and to be in its flow, we need to stop resisting and just go with and into the flow. Everything is about timing. Believing my car space will be there when I am, is me, trusting I have nothing to worry about.

Life is much easier to navigate if you *move into the flow*. This doesn't mean you're lazy, No! It means that you're tired of the struggle and tired of feeling as if you have to do it all alone. When you don't! It might sound a little weird to you, that I trust my life like this, but it works for me and I feel so much freer as a result.

My intuition and I became a very good team and my team is much bigger than just my intuition and I. Think of your Guardian Angels, Ascended Masters (people, who have lived and taught on this earth to help mankind, and then returned *home*, to their spirit form), and the God within. This is all I'm going to say about that right now.

I really want you to enjoy reading about my road trip. Although it is quite obvious, as we go along, that my systems of belief have been challenged and they and I've changed from where I was then, to where I'm now. You may find that some of my belief systems challenge your belief systems, and where you are. I want you to know that I honour and respect that. I also have to believe that if you're reading this, there is a reason for it.

What I'm saying is that trust in anything or anyone can take time. Time will prove to you whether your trust has been misplaced, and time provides you with tangible *proof.* Let's be honest. We all want proof, before we commit to a relationship, a new job, going to a party or whatever is uppermost in your thoughts at the time. We always get an *instinct*; a first thought that gives us a feeling about someone, and about something. It is this feeling that we can choose to ignore, or not.

That instinct is the proof we want, although sometimes we ignore that proof. Why? Because we want what we want, and then time proves to us, what our first instinct or thought was telling us, in a way we cannot ignore or shut out. Don't feel bad if you're remembering a situation where this applies. Let's face it! You can also have a lot of fun with your bad choice. Although, I also bet that you – that all of us – learnt some very important lessons that we needed to learn along the way.

These lessons can have a very positive effect in our life, as we move forward. Some lessons come in very enticing packages, be it people or projects. Now is the time to start to learn to recognise what the *signs,* which signal trust, are for you, and which are those that signal mistrust? Unless you don't want to, and that's fine too, but then you should have bought a different book. I'm only kidding.

*****

My father had been gone for about nine months and my life had really become unstuck since he'd left. In my heart I knew my marriage was destined to end. When? I didn't have that information. I only knew that the day would come and it would just happen, like rotten fruit finally falling from the tree, and all you can feel is saddened by the waste.

It was a weekday and the children were still in school and preschool. I was outside hanging out the washing, when I got the feeling I should go inside and sit down in the lounge room. I finished outside and this persistent thought was still in my head. I went inside and sat down in the lounge room. Then the feeling turned into a voice that got louder and stronger...

"Bring pen and paper for Dad's visits."

Blindly accepting this, I rushed out to get a pen and my note pad. I sat down again and waited.

"Dad if this is you, please let me know? I've missed you so much," I said.

Within seconds, I started writing and writing. A lot of people call this automatic writing. I guess that is a good description, because for me the writing came from somewhere else, with no conscious thought on my part.

Over the years I can feel when it is my soul speaking to me, and at other times there have been numerous spirits, angels etc. I know this because my actual handwriting when I'm writing them is very different to how I write myself. Sometimes it slants backwards and is very large and other time it looks pretty and flowing, a bit like calligraphy – something I really want to learn one day.

Learning through the
Brotherhood of Beings   12.9.18

A Star seed living & breathing on
a dense planet to experience
feelings unlike those of the
higher realms.

Feelings & emotions contains subtles
that bring about greater & a different
depth of learning

Your system (the Earth System)
is the training ground for new
Angelic Beings who will contain
a greater depth of understanding than
those who have choosen to
remain in the astral realm.

It is in the new class room
where both these energies will bring
& share knowledge with
each other then astral & earthly
energies will learn a different
style of being

a Different Style of Being

Bring forth with this love a new and nurturing circle of love ever ready to meet the needs placed upon it for its strength eminates from its wisdom, gained through the ages, and now unlocked, ~~and~~ flowing freely to cleanse the waters, muddied by eons of pain, hurt & humiliation. Look up and see the beauty that is lovingly called "the truth". The truth which is talked about often but so seldom released for fear of pain. Can you not now see the wisdom in truth

166

However, this day I knew it was my dad. Not so much from the style of writing, but rather from the content. The voice and tone were exactly like our café coffee chats used to be. When I read what was written down, I cried because I didn't feel so alone anymore. Dad told me that he would always be watching over us and would stay for as long as he felt the children and I needed him. He said to believe him when he told me that we would be happy again one day.

From that day on, my dad came to our writing sessions, not every day but sometimes once a week, and sometimes more. Each time filled me with strength and hope for a future that didn't include pain, at least not the kind I'd become used to. Then one day, about two years later Dad stopped coming. It was after my divorce was final and I was packing to move north.

When I realised this, I felt the grief all over again. I couldn't understand why he had left when I still needed him. Eventually, I came to understand. You have to do some things for yourself. I could have had as much support as possible, but unless I went through it, whatever it was or is how would I to find the inner strength to grow and move forward in my life.

I needed to know, really know, that I had that kind of strength. I need to prove to myself that I could do what seemed impossible at the time. I knew I needed great courage and strength to overcome a kind of fear that not all of us have to face. The kind of fear that nothing could ever really prepare me for. Dad's leaving was a great lesson, so I could find out about myself and, when I needed it most of all, I had it.

After a while, I started writing again, mainly for myself, and occasionally someone new turned up to speak to me through the writing space. I had been through a lot, but I didn't feel lonely when I was by myself anymore and I wasn't upset that Dad had stopped our writing sessions. It was just life. Life always keeps on moving and now I could keep moving with it.

Thanks to my dad, it felt normal when my conversations with spirits started, even though it also felt somehow different to the times before. The times I spent in this space were so natural, so full of light, of love, and so full of God. The voice was the purest voice I've ever heard and I never thought to question, but I did begin to ask questions. I was open and, in full faith, I accepted the purity of the voice and the words that came to me, through me. This is one of those pieces from August.

*****

"Oh dear one you do not see the love all around you. Happenstance and love have led you here. The time is right for you now. Let love guide you and your thoughts will be guided by us.

Trying to think is not needed or necessary. Let our love lead the way to a place where peace on earth is the reality for all. We understand the reality you think is unattainable, but this year we have enacted many things that people needed to learn. Peace within the heart will give peace to those who see more. A people who have nothing else have peace and love, if left alone.

Sometimes help is needed and sometimes help is misguided. This, your planet has been disturbed so that those who always chose to live within its seasons were looked after. While those who tried to disrupt the seasons did more damage due to their understanding of what is right and what is needed.

Listen to the children of the world, many of whom have already left. For the energy you were disrupting made it hard for them to continue, through tears of frustration.

You are all in for a shock soon, as the world takes a further tumble off its course and the reason for your being. You were sent here to bring selfless love, but the greed of a few, as we have seen throughout years of earth's centuries has cost many lives and the price is too much.

Love, not greed can bring you back. Each of you has the power, for the voices of the many are to rise and keep rising against the few who strive and struggle to keep the past in the present.

If you are to bring the earth's energy up to the vibration of its highest-level occupants, then there is a chance of turning love into the inventor. But, those who now feel the world is there for their plundering must be brought to justice, in the Court of Humanity for their crimes against what they purport to embrace.

More and more Masters have left and are leaving your world, their gifts (knowledge) to your world extended. When riches, love and energy are given and revered then left to lie alone in cupboards with other unused items, then those who have been given the chance to better humanity and not taken it will burn within their own bodies.

Know we are watching, always watching, and waiting for the thoughts of children to be cherished and embraced in a new world order.

Help because help is needed, not because you must take responsibility for its location."

*****

When people started to seek me out for *readings,* I didn't feel right about doing them because – at that stage... didn't feel I was doing what psychics or clairvoyants do. Certainly not the ones I had been to or had read about or seen on television and at the seminars they gave. Sure, I could tell you about love, health, wealth and career, which is what the majority of people want to know about. They are the usual things we think about, sometimes constantly, if we're not where we think we ought to be *by now.*

But, this wasn't the priority of what I would have coming through for them. It really took a while for me to understand what it was I was actually doing. I finally understood when a client asked me "How does this work? How do you do what you do?" I started to explain that it seems never to be the same. It changes depending who comes to see me.

The information I give out is purely spirit-based and I'm guided to respond in the way your spirit knows will help you the most at the time. Sometimes, I'm guided to use cards, which draw me to different images in a collage of pictures. I may get many things for you to ingest and sit with in your own space. Other times the cards stay on the table and the whole session is channelled. If this happens, I rarely remember the words coming through, although the feelings or images I get may stay with me a bit longer.

*****

How did I begin to trust, and to truly believe in and use my intuition? As I've said, playing games is the quickest way to test and recognise when you 'get it right', plus it's fun. The more you get it right, the more your trust increases and your belief multiplies. Pick anything to start with. For me, it was number plates, radar, and parking spaces, because I've always done a lot of driving.

You might work in a shop, so try to figure out what the next customer will be like, or what colour they will be wearing. There are so many things to use when testing your own intuition. To do this, take a few deep breaths to focus your mind, and then ask a question; for example, *what colour will my next customer be wearing?* Then let it go and trust the first image or word that comes to mind. You may not get it right the first time, but the more you keep doing this the easier it will become.

If you haven't used your mind this way before, if you were studying, we could say this would be, *Breath Mind Connection 101.* You get what I'm saying. Everything begins with the basics, and in this area they are the connection you make between breathing and the thoughts that come once you're centred, so that a connection can be made to your inner self.

This is about listening, and resisting the impulse to let the normal thoughts, which fill your mind every day, intrude. Use your breath to slow everything down. The voice of your soul, the God source, the essence of your soul will become stronger with practice and a great way to begin is through meditation.

I first started to notice that the thoughts I was interested in the most were the ones that I saw flick across my eyes. It happened too quickly for me to understand what they were really about, but slow enough for me to know they were important to me in some way.

How could I pull these thoughts from my subconscious and into my conscious mind, from where I could take a good look at them, and expand them until I could clearly see what it was about and what it meant to my surroundings and me? Eventually the more I practiced the more natural it felt to do.

****

Channelling became a natural progression from where I was, to where I seemed to be going and one through which the love and purity of spirit, of the God source, could come through. Once I started asking questions, I began to understand this light-filled pure voice was not meant to be a secret between us. It was not meant to be hidden. Yet, I had been hiding in my invisibility most of my life.

Nothing else had ever resonated so strongly. Finally, I understood what my role was, what the gift was I bought to share – helping others learn how to listen to that voice within. To trust, accept and acknowledge their pure light and the loving voice of the God within. Yes, we all have the power to do this for ourselves. It does not matter how much or how little, as long as you're aware of its existence within you and know that it is there to help guide you through your life, using whatever gift you brought to share with the rest of us.

This was to be a big challenge for me, as I had to overcome my fear of being visible again. But my gift was meant to be shared and talked about in the open light of day. All I wanted to do was to help others, by opening up to the messages coming through for those of you who wanted and needed their questions answered.

This knowledge is there for all human beings to access, if they so choose and it starts with listening. Go to that quiet space where your breathing connects you to the centre of your soul, the essence of your soul, and listen... just listen.

*****

Your Soul Essence is the sum total of all the knowledge and wisdom your spirit has accumulated throughout the many eons of its existence;

It is the God source that brings love to all that you are and all that you will ever be.

It is the knowing and intangible part of you, the part that celebrates in your greatest moments of joy and the soft whispered voice of compassion that gives you strength in your deepest moments of despair.

It is the **Source of God** that brings love to all that you are and all you will ever be... **It is LOVE.**

This is where all the answers to all the questions you have or will ever have are waiting to be discovered by you. Do not be afraid. Ask, and then stay still and quiet enough to hear.

*****

The God Source resides within in each living being, no matter how big or small. For eons, we have looked to the God outside of ourselves. We have called him/her by many names throughout the ages and within different cultures, and all of us profess to do his/her work. We have become used to using the name of God as a weapon, instead of a guiding light to show us the way to living in heaven on earth.

We have asked for things, and we've questioned him/her. We have demanded and have laid blame at his/her feet when things haven't worked out the way we wanted them to. However, as human *beings,* we've never taken responsibility for our actions and the destruction our undertakings have brought to the earth, on which we need to live in our human state.

When are we going to start listening? And if we do, to whom do we listen? We listen to the God within, who wants peace, compassion, and kindness towards all our fellow human beings. We listen to our children, who are closer to the God within and who will stay so and keep listening, unless we try to change their thoughts, and their thinking. They trust us, because they know no other way. Can we not trust and believe in them, and what they have to offer and teach us?

*" If you allow light to shine your way,
you will see perfection in each new day.
You will see
there is nothing but perfection !"*

CHAPTER 9

The Believing

For me, the believing comes when I witness or feel something for myself. I am a trusting kind of person. If you tell me something, I will believe it, whatever that something is, until there is proof to the contrary. Who am I to say another person's experiences are true or false? If a psychic tells me things about my life, I know if it is true, whether it resonates with me or whether it is something no one else could know.

When you go to a psychic, there is an energy that merges, if you're willing. If you want a reading you must allow your walls, your energetic walls, to come down long enough for the drapes to be drawn back on the subconscious and your higher spiritual intelligence.

As I mentioned earlier, my Dad left one day, about two years after he and I had been communicating (between worlds/the doorway). He told me I didn't need him anymore and in one way this was true. He had already helped me get through so much. But, it felt so final. I think his leaving me on this level allowed me to truly grieve, and grieve I did. For a long, long, time I felt lost without his kind supportive voice in my head.

Eventually though, I realised he had to go and do what spirits do over there. Because time is not linear where he is, I only have to think of him now and he is here. Even when I'm not thinking about him sometimes I will feel his essence around. The same goes for my mom, only she is harder to get in touch with. She is so happy where she is and, like her younger self, she gets to fly like the wind without her fragile, tired body to hold her down.

This does not have to be anyone else's view, but knowing there is no true death frees me in such a peace-filled way. Oh, I still have my moments of grieving the physical loss of those I love; my mom, my dad and the tiny soul I lost so long ago. The physical loss never really leaves. It hides itself away, deep in my heart, until a feathered touch of recognition or a song brings my loss to the surface and my grief is undeniable again, for a while.

But, this is life. This is life in all its colours: The glory and the grief. Who am I to try to deny either one? Our own free will allows us to experience whatever it is we want to experience, while we live in this physical world. This is the world of the tangible, a world of feeling and fighting, a world of love and purpose, a world of loss and emptiness. Do your best or do your worst, while you're here. This is where we learn about all of these feelings, but most of all this is where we can learn about compassion and forgiveness and self-worth and self-love.

*****

I wish to share another story with you. It happened a few months after we had settled in Palm Beach.

I found myself in the middle of Bloomingdale's Department Store in New York City, with a friend. We were there to attend a fundraiser, but before we did, I needed a belt. I heard a small child cry out, terrified, In the next aisle. I looked over to witness a mother hitting her small child with a belt. This pain sent an arrow through my heart. I started to rush around to protect the child. At the same moment felt a hand restrain me.

My girlfriend and the sales woman who'd been helping us intervened and took me away. They sat me in the corner near the register and away from the scene taking place. I couldn't breathe. I was shaking and overwhelmed with pain that sobbed out of every pore of my skin, as my friend and the sales lady tried to make me understand why I could not get involved. I heard nothing of what they were saying.

My spirit released and had other ideas. I flew to the child's side and took the mother's hand in mine. I looked into her eyes.

"I recognise your pain. Hit me!"

The witnesses around saw nothing of the agreement between us, but my spirit stood there amongst them, in front of her child as I faced the mother. I took each stroke of the belt until her anger subsided and the child behind me felt safe. As the mother and child walked away, I watched the child reach up to hold her mother's hand. People went about their busy day and I returned to my body on the chair in the corner, until the pain subsided.

This was the first time I had *astral travelled* during the day. I thought about the impact it had upon me physically, later that night, as I stood in the bathroom of the hotel room. I realised no silver cord had been attached. Maybe I didn't need it any more. Maybe it had been an earlier tool I needed when starting out on test runs, so to speak, to give me the confidence to try this astral travelling thing?

There was a knock at the door.

"Karen, are you alright? You've been in there for a while now, I was starting to worry," my friend said.

"Yes, I'm fine. You can come in," I replied. She opened the door.

"Can you help me?" I asked. "I can't see the back. Could you straighten it up a bit for me?"

"Oh my God! Karen! What have you done?" she asked shocked.

I looked at all my hair lying on the bathroom floor. "It was too heavy," I said as I handed her the scissors.

After some travelling on the West Coast, we arrived home and I threw the best Halloween party ever. Oh, and if you're wondering about my children, my friend's adult/daughter stayed at my place and looked after them while I was gone. She was actually a nanny. The Halloween costumes I'd bought the children put the biggest smiles on their faces and life returned to our *new* normal.

Note: Later, as we were enjoying a cuppa and looking at the photos I'd taken of our trip, my girlfriend told me that the sales woman in New York had said to her, "There was no way anyone would get involved to help the little girl in the department store because the woman and her child were African American. They don't get involved in each other's business."

"I don't understand, I don't understand."

I've never really noticed the outer shell of people. I seem to connect more with and recognise the soul of a person. It really didn't matter anyway. Whatever business she, the little girl, and I had was honoured in spirit, and had been completed by us. It was on the path of forgiveness and no one else's business.

*****

Forgiveness comes from having compassion for another and from being able to recognise what they may be feeling. Sometimes we can and sometimes we can't or won't. Either way it is all about the choices each one of us makes while we're here, and about learning to take responsibility for where these choices lead us.

Laying blame on others is a way of not looking at or dealing with the hurt inside of us. If we can find it in our heats to forgive another, then maybe we can find the courage in our hearts to forgive ourselves. If we can do this, then maybe we can move away from all the guilt and start heading towards living our best life possible, whatever that is for you and me.

What is your best life?

How do you see yourself in the living of it?

What kind of things do you see yourself doing in your life?

What do you truly want to do and how does it feel when you are doing it?

Take a few moments now, to think about how you really would like your life to look. Get a note pad and write down some of the things you feel when you think about these questions. What images come into your mind? Can you see where you're in your new life adventure? For those of you who like *Vision Boards*, start making one. Get a canvas and start cutting out things, pictures, and words that apply to the life you want to start creating. Begin today!

My Vision Board

Once you finish your **Vision Board,** place it in your home. It has to go somewhere you will see it and notice it every day, so that consciously and subconsciously you will be reinforcing the positive and happy thoughts it generates, every time you see it. But, DON'T put it on the back of the toilet door where all your good work will be flushed away... every time you see it! You can also make it your screen saver on your phone. Your mind is the most powerful ally you have. Use it to help you feel great about where you choose to go and leave the grief and negative thoughts far behind.

Devote your thoughts to thinking positively about the life you want to live in. From this moment on, let all negative feelings, you may harbour against yourself or others, go. Because whether you believe it or not, those thoughts have got you to the place in your life where you are right now. If you're already living your best life possible, that's wonderful and exciting for you.

BUT, if you're not in a happy place and are not feeling free and content with where your life is going; if you sometimes think "*This can't be it. This can't be all there is?*" then let them go! They haven't served your best interests. They haven't got you where you want to be yet, have they? Get rid of them today, right now in this minute and never look back at them again. Don't give them time in your day. Not anymore!

Now, you're probably thinking, but it's just not that easy to do. For the most part you would be right. What *do* I do? What can I do to get rid of negativity when it comes up? This is a very good question, and one I'll answer. I mean, let's face it, you already know a lot about me and I've messed up plenty, so I'm not going to sit here and tell you it's as easy to do as that.

Snap your fingers and it just disappears. It did take some work for me and it will take some work for you, too. But, aren't you worth it?

What is one way to get rid of those negative nuisance thoughts?

"Your vision helps you to see.
The board helps you to hope.
Creating allows you to dream.
Doing brings it into your reality."

Your Vision Board. Keep your focus on moving forward and don't be so hard on yourself, if you slip into negativity. It will get less and less. When you start putting things on your Vision Board is the perfect time to start trusting that the signs are out there to help guide you to your most perfect life. All you need to do is to begin to recognise them. They could be small signs, or big signs (like my billboard, talk about in your face).

If you believe the signs are there, you can literally trip over them. We all have our own triggers that let us know when something is good for us or not. Learn what yours are, test them, learn to trust them and then believe in them. Believe that they will keep guiding you forward, if you keep listening, noticing, and believing.

No second guessing. They will guide you in the best direction for you. Truth be told, you probably have a good idea of what, at least, some of yours are already.

If, after doing all of this, maybe you're still not feeling good about a choice you made and where it took you. This doesn't just have to be about that big life choice. "What do I want to do with the *REST* of my life?" It can be the smallest decision, but at least start making them. Your life is going to happen with or without you making the choices in it. Don't become inert about your life, or you'll get to the end and realise you only sat on the sidelines, petrified, and then became 'petrified'...

I was given an early example of these signs at my first Hay House one-day seminar. There were various speakers on the program, all of whom I had either read their books or had been told about by other friends, who were also attending that day. I had driven over to my mum's early that morning, as my children were to spend the day with her while I was at the seminar, as its location, The Horden Pavilion, was close to her home.

Just before I arrived at Mum's, I turned the corner and saw a car that had the same colour and make as a man/child I had been seeing a few months before. The number plate on this car was CURSE. I was astounded as it really felt like a curse at the time.

After I arrived at the seminar, I saw a couple of people I knew. We were all seated listening to the first speaker, who was talking about Feng Shui. After that, Dr. Wayne W. Dyer was introduced. The next two hours flew by as he spoke. I had read some of his books and they had resonated with me, so I was listening to his words intently. At one point, he spoke about soul mates, and said we connect with our soul family. Through them we learn and we teach each other the lessons we need or wish to learn.

"Not all soul mates are of the romantic kind," Wayne said. "Sometimes it is the CURSE on your shoulder that teaches you through pain." I nearly fell off my chair. I wasn't even looking for signs, but here was a big one. One that apparently someone didn't want me to miss.

That is not so much intuition, but spirit making sure I get the message it's trying to give me. That message for me was SELF-WORTH! I really did need to start believing in myself and valuing who I was!

"Learn your true worth.
Do not be afraid!
Place value on yourself,
and then others will too!"

Sometimes it is like this. Sometimes you can quite literally trip over a sign, if it is in your best interests to do so. But, you need to be aware that there are signs all around you, around us, but nothing can help to guide you, if you're not open to that possibility. Testing your intuition and learning to trust your intuition will get you to the point where it becomes so natural to do that. There are no questions and you use it every day without thinking about it.

This is when you learn to believe, not only in the existence of intuition or gut instinct but also to the point of never leaving home without it, so to speak.

However, not all *signs* are visible. They could be a thought in your mind or they might come as a very strong feeling about something. You could overhear a word or sentence in a conversation between two strangers, or something on the side of a bus jumps out at you. A car overtakes you and instead of getting angry, you look at the number plate and notice that numbers or letters, or both mean something to you. Just to you and no one else. The list goes on and on.

However signs still require your being able to believe in them. By now, you're probably well on your way to doing this. Being conscious of signs, and of our feelings and how they speak to us about them is unique and very important. For example, if I'm doing a reading for someone, or even having a chat with a girlfriend, and I get cold, like freezing cold, goose bumps and all, this tells me that what I'm saying to them, at that exact moment, is an absolute truth for them.

I know this for sure through my many years of working with clients and the feedback I've received over that time. It doesn't have to be about something huge either. But, when it happens I have no doubts. It is all the confirmation I need. I might get a cold shiver; you know the ones that feel like someone just walked over your grave. When this happens, it warns me that something needs a little more investigation, and depending on what is being said at the time, it is usually pretty clear what needs to be done.

Other times, I've found myself quite literally choking, when I was reading for someone. It turned out that the person who was sitting across from me had some things she wanted to address in her relationship, but every time she went to say something, she couldn't get her words out. We looked at this and after some discussion, she made a decision for herself, and felt strong enough to talk with her partner.

I don't know whether she did. But, she told me that witnessing me choking like that made her realise she was not helping herself or her partner by letting things go on as they were.

Another time, as soon as the person sat down across from me I felt myself getting very emotional, which I try not to do, as it doesn't seem very professional. After a few minutes, I felt a strong energy in the space with us. Without thinking, I asked her if someone very close to her had passed over recently.

"Yes they have."

"I can feel a motherly energy around you. Your mother wants you to know that she will be there, when her grandchild is born and to be brave because she knows you will get through this. She will be by your side the whole way," I said.

The woman started to cry and told me what had happened.

"My mother died very suddenly and we're all in shock. My baby is, was going to be her first grandchild."

"I'm sorry," I said. "It is hard to lose your mother at any age, but at this time I can understand just how hard it must be for you. Remember what she said to you, here today. Hold it in your heart and take strength knowing she is watching over you and her grandchild... and don't be afraid to let people in."

These are just a couple of examples where believing in what you do comes by working with the signs and symbols that hold significance for you. They don't need confirmation from another person to prove to you that they are right. Very probably that other person will think you are, at the very least, a bit weird. So, I say keep your weirdness to yourself. Don't give others a chance to rain on your parade, or to pull you down when you're feeling up or excited about your new discovery. Your discovery is yours alone. Treat it like a secret and care for it like the precious object it is. Value the significance of it in your life, and be excited at how this is going to play out for you.

I know I get excited when something happens for me. Maybe it is something that others would not understand, or maybe they would understand all too well. We live in Australia and we're known for what is referred to as the 'Tall Poppy Syndrome'. We don't need to be visible to others. As you begin this new journey, you're embarking upon, nurture it until you're truly ready to take some hard knocks from people who may not understand why or what you need to do for yourself and your life.

However, once you're ready, shine away. Let your brightness light up the sky. Because by then, it won't matter what others say. You will be confident in yourself as you are and able to accept the compliments along with the critique. When you're living the life of your choice, all else falls away. You can speak with confidence through your soul.

*****

I actually I did stop *listening* for a while. This was after I had been doing psychic work for about ten years, at the football club, and more years doing psychic fairs and special events etc. I don't know exactly when I stopped. It wasn't even a conscious choice. One day, I just didn't have the energy. I had become overwhelmed. There was too much going on in my life with my family. Something had to give. I didn't have the energy to do both at that time, or so I thought...

Your psychic ability never truly goes away, and when I was ready, I woke up to the sounds of the psychic within me again. It was as simple as that. All I needed to do was, listen. This was proven to me during a group meditation. At some point in the meditation, I felt a hand on my right shoulder. I turn my head to see Kuthumi. He had become my spiritual teacher and guide after my dad left. He felt like a very old and comfortable friend.

"You're back!" I exclaimed.

"I never left you" he said to me.

It was then that I understood that our guides are always with us, but they cannot interfere unless we ask them to, or pray for their help. It's a freewill thing. We can choose to ask for guidance. or we can choose to hobble along without it. It really is up to each of us how we decide we want to live. It's a bit like needing a new pair of glasses. Do you struggle along pretending the ones you have are just fine, or do you ask your optometrist to help you chose new ones? That is, you ask for help, get the tools you need and get on with the job of living. It really is that simple.

"Allowing fear to stop you living,
is about as silly as
trying to stop a wave with your hands.
Grab a surfboard.
Enjoy the ride!"

204

CHAPTER 10

The Knowing

My conscious choice to stop doing *readings* etc. was what actually helped me get to the *knowing* part. By not *turning them on* to do a *reading,* I came to realise that, over the years, I had learned how to function this way automatically. Even though I thought I had *turned them off,* now, I hadn't. It actually had the opposite effect.

Now, the difference is I was functioning automatically and subconsciously with my intuitive abilities throughout my day-to-day life. I came to recognise that when the conscious and subconscious work hand-in-hand, we function as a fully-integrated human and spiritual being.

Lifting our senses to a higher plane, a higher frequency, feels even more natural, and is more in keeping with who we are. An easy example of how this works is this. A dog can hear what we cannot, such as the sound of a whistle at a certain pitch that only animals can hear.

It is the same with psychics. They can hear at a particular frequency, a higher vibration than you can. But, by using your intuitive abilities you can continually enhance them to the point of *knowing* they are and will be there for you to use. They are an integral part of you. I'm not saying that this can make you a psychic. That might not be your chosen purpose. What I'm saying is that you can use what you know, to enhance your decision-making to get you to your most-perfect life, via a lighter, brighter path.

I've always said, and will keep on saying, that there are no coincidences. It is my belief that everything happens for a reason, but you're probably getting sick of me saying this. However, while all of this psychic thing was coming back for me, I still had two young children to look after. Anyone who has children knows you very rarely get time to yourself alone. When you do, it's most likely because they are tucked up in bed sound asleep. Then, you find yourself doing everything you need to do to get ready for the next day and then heading straight under the covers, to get whatever sleep you can before they wake you up... again.

Of course, after they got older and were both in school I was able to work again. It was a choice I made. We had all been through so much. Earlier on, I knew my children needed my presence more than any small luxuries my working could have given them. However, working and having children was so different and it was much more important for me to be able to fit both together, as any mother knows all too well.

As I said there are no coincidences. So, how did I learn to live in the physical part of my world, while trying to embrace the psychic part of me, to the extent where I felt complete and whole? I kept looking and trusting that something would come to me that honoured where I saw my future choices taking me. As usual it happened in the most unusual way.

*****

It happened a couple of years after we had moved to Palm Beach, and from there on to Whale Beach. Our local market was on and I decided to take a stall. I had just finished writing a small poetry book and I decided to set up at the market to sell it.

The night before the market, a friend suggested, "Karen why don't you do your readings at the stall as well?"

"No," I replied. "I don't feel ready to do them for a fee yet, and people seem to expect a certain kind of 'psychic'. I'm not like any of the ones I've ever been to."

"Well I think it's a waste of an opportunity, and what have you got to lose. You could charge them $3 for three minutes!" She laughed.

"That's a great idea." I said.

"Are you serious, Karen?" she asked.

"Yes absolutely. It will kill the time and if they don't like how I do it then it's only $3. I won't feel guilty and they shouldn't feel ripped off! It's a win-win. Now quick, let's make up a sign before I get cold feet."

The next morning came and the sun was out... no rain for me. I pulled up at the market gate and asked directions to my stall, which was in a very good place between the lake and Pittwater Road, Narrabeen. I knew there would be a lot of people going through. I emptied my car, and carried my table, chair and sign over to start setting up. A third trip back to the car to get one more box of books and I was finally ready to start my day.

In the first hour I had sold three books and was pretty happy. A few friends dropped by to say hello. One girlfriend bought me a cuppa from the Coffee Van for which I was grateful and a breakfast roll, which I couldn't eat. I realised early on that I was not able to eat before I did readings, especially if I was booked for an event, or a party, but mostly at the football club, where I worked for ten years. I will tell you about this later. Then, the people started wandering through. It was a beautiful day and I was happy just to sit and read a book, if that was all that happened that day. But, this was not the case.

First one person came and asked for a reading. I always feel a little bit nervous, before I start, as I never know what is going to come through. However once I begin, I'm in a different place and the time just flies by. About half an hour later, someone else came, and his reading was about ten minutes, so any guilty feelings I had about value for money went out the window. My three-minute readings were turning into ten, sometimes fifteen minutes. Later I had to learn how to start and stop in the allotted timeframe, which was always a challenge for me.

Then, all of a sudden, I had people queuing up, waiting for when I was free. It was a crazy day, but I was having fun. That is until I started to find a theme running through all of these readings. I realised that I could hear myself saying practically the same thing at every one of them. I was starting to sound like a fraud, even to my own ears. I prayed no one was around listening to what I was saying. I knew I wasn't, yet each of these people, male and female, felt the same things; anger, frustration, and sadness. It was nothing major but most, if not all of them, seemed really unhappy with where their lives were at the moment.

At 4:00pm, when the market closed, I had only two people who felt happy and their readings had been really enjoyable for me to do. One was a shop owner, who had also asked if I could come and work in her shop one day a week. I was thrilled to say yes, and I went to see her before I left for home. The other was a lovely young woman. When she came to me, straight away I could feel her happiness and I told her so.

The reading I did for her was so uplifting. She was very happy with where she was in her life, and only wanted confirmation that the choice she was about to make was good for her. I told her it was the best choice she could make for herself at this time. After a few more minutes, we finished. I felt happier than I'd felt all day and I told her that.

"I'm so glad you came to see me. I've had a day where just about everyone who came to see me, felt the same way and were at a similar place in their lives. I thought I was going crazy. It seems so ridiculous," I explained.

She said, "Oh no you're right. Everyone in my family has been coming over to have a reading. They think you're amazing. Each time someone came back and told us what you said another one came over to see you."

I turned to look as she pointed out her family. Yep! They were all there waving to me. I laughed so hard, it finally made sense. I was not going crazy and I stopped doubting my ability.

I went home happy and exhausted and began eating anything I had in my fridge. I was ravenous. After I had had enough to eat, I sat down to count my earning for the day. Three books and 27 readings: total $112.30. I went to sleep exhausted and happy that I had finally charged for my readings, even if my price was ridiculous, and, that people were very happy with what came through for them. It gave me confidence and that, it appeared, was all I needed.

I started working in the little shop, for the woman from the markets, and I had it to myself each Wednesday. Sometimes, I would get two or three customers wanting a reading throughout the day. I started at 10:00am and finished at 02:00pm, whether anyone came in or not. I was doing readings for 30 minutes now, but not for $3.

On a slow morning, a woman came into see me. She seemed very proper and was dressed up as if she was going to a show or some kind of event. She sat down in the chair before I even had a chance to say hello. Are you here for a reading?

"Of course I am. Why else would I be here?" she said.

"Alright that's fine," I said as I sat down behind my table and we began. I used a 'Voyager' pack of tarot cards in my readings. I didn't really need them, but sometimes people expected to see them and sometimes I found that the information came through quicker with them. I'll explain about how I came by these cards, shortly.

I shuffled the cards, and then I put them face down on the table. Usually people will take somewhere between three to seven cards. I asked the woman to take a few cards from the top.

She grabbed more than half the deck, glared at me, and said, "You can tell me what's in these." I didn't know whether to laugh or cry. Surely, she couldn't be serious. It would take me all day.

I met her challenge. I put the rest of the pack away, and took the cards from her to begin. After ten minutes, she said quite gruffly "Alright! Alright! I know all this. Tell me something I don't know."

I laughed to myself, because it is usually the other way around. Most people want you to tell them things they know, so it proves to them that you can do what you say you can.

If she thought I was going to give in to her defiant demeanour, she was mistaken. I found the courage to say something to her, which I've never felt the need to say to anyone else I've read for. I took a deep breath, stood my ground so to speak, and said, "I understand if you're not happy. I will end the reading now and there will be no charge." I went to stand up when she stopped me.

"No, no, you can keep going," she said.

"For me to continue, you will need to let down the block that you've put up," I said to her. "It is impossible for me to continue otherwise." All the bluffness and posturing left her and she felt quite small and fragile.

"Thank You. Shall we continue?" I said. The rest of the reading was a joy for us both. I felt I had really helped and she was very happy as we parted.

As I've said before I don't believe in coincidences and the reading I did with that woman taught me a valuable lesson. That was to trust and believe in myself more, and to trust in what I was feeling at the time and to be true to those feelings and not afraid to speak up. That reading helped my confidence greatly, and allowed me to give the best of myself through what I do. It also enabled me to help someone, which is all I want to do. We both walked away from it feeling better than when we'd started.

Since that day, I've done readings for many people from all walks of life, and it has been a joy for me to help those who came to me. It is a privilege and an honour to be of service to others. When I'm doing readings I feel so grateful that I have this gift and am able to share it with them. And I do mean share.

I always take something away from these readings for myself. Something that my guides, my angels, and other beings that help enhance what I do when it is needed. It is one way they communicate with me, especially if I'm being stubborn. By stubborn I mean not making the time to listen to my inner voice, when it calls to me, because of the normal day-to-day things that I allow to get in the way.

As I've said before, I live in the physical world just as you do. Sometimes it is easier for them to tell me something through a reading that I do for another, because I listen, so that I can give my client the answers directly, as they come from spirit through me. Mostly nothing makes sense to me, nor is it supposed to, as it is not for me. However, sometimes, and only sometimes, they make sure I hear what they are saying.

Of course, I only come to understand this after the actual reading, and the way I understand this is because I don't remember what I said to the person sitting across from me. I'm not meant to. However, when I'm sitting quietly after a reading, some fragments of what was said will slip back into my mind. This is how I know there was also a message for me.

*"Whatever the question,
the answer is always yes!
This you know, before you even ask.
It is your truth,
seeking a way of expression."*

CHAPTER 11

Guidance

Workshop: I decided it was time to hold a workshop. I wanted to run a workshop, as an introduction to helping people who wanted to learn how to access their own intuitive abilities. I had been putting a lot of thought into how this could best work and had come up with an idea that I loved. The day of my first workshop was almost here and I was so excited. I had done a lot of work to get to a point, where I felt comfortable providing this service to others. After all, who was I to be giving advice?

My life had been a ridiculous mess for most of its length. However, I found that I had actually learnt something from my experiences over the years and maybe I might be able to help someone else, because of what I learnt through them. I was certainly going to give it a try. Here I was; with an incredible group of women, who were open to hearing what I had to say and willing to give it a go. It meant so much to me.

What I also hoped to do in these workshops was to explain a little of how I came to be doing this and why. I wanted to share some of the tools I'd used that had helped me. I wanted others to see if they could use these, if they wanted to try embracing their intuition in their lives. I hoped to help them see that intuition is just another sense and one that can be used to guide one along one's life path.

In these workshops, I told the participants this. Just for this one day, I would like you to be open to trusting that your intuition is ready and willing to help guide you to where you want to be in your life. It is jumping for a chance to help guide you and to enable you to have the best life you can. If you're like me, you will want some kind of proof that it truly exists in you and not just in 'other people'.

This was why I put the workshops together and why I'm writing this book for you, now. Just like in those workshops, I know that if you want to find it, you will.

How did the workshop begin? I had a set plan for how I wanted to run the day. I had prepared workbooks to give to the participants on arrival. Although I knew other things would take the day in different directions, this was the part I loved the best. I was living in what I like to call the tree house; a beautiful older wooden building surrounded by bamboo and banana trees that kept it cool in summer. This lovely home had a wall of windows overlooking 'The Pittwater', a fabulous waterway on the Northern Beaches of Sydney. It was the perfect serene setting for the day we were about to embark on.

There were five women in our group, six including me, although over the years these groups grew much larger and included men as well. Introductions were made and then we all sat down on the lounge chairs I had arranged so that we faced each other. I welcomed them into the space.

I always start with a short meditation and prayer, which takes you out of the business of your daily life. It helps centre your thoughts and brings your energy into the sacred space we create between us and hold for the work we do that day. It is very important to do this, as our energy runs high during the session while we're learning and practicing what we've learned. For this reason, space must be created to keep us balanced throughout the day. Plus, it is a wonderful space to be in. it is filled with the fun and excitement of learning something about yourself that you may not already know.

The world, all our worlds, do not exist in this space. It has only us in it. What we're trying to do for ourselves is to deepen our intuition and to focus this skill for use in our day-to-day lives. This is very important, because once we conclude our day – excited and enjoying where it took us – the minute we step back into our day-to-day lives, especially those of you with children your focus goes off yourself and back to those whom you love, and who depend on you, as well as what 'needs' to be done.

You know what I'm saying here, don't you? However, the workshop is the time for you to work out when, how, and where you can fit what you've learned into your everyday life. It may take some time to truly integrate this into your life, although I can promise you this. Once done you will recognise how important and relevant it is for that you to continue trusting you're doing something extremely important for yourself and something that will flow on positively to those you love, as well.

For example, when I'm talking with my young granddaughter, I find my intuition really helps me to understand her and to be totally present with her. It helps me listen when she wants to talk about whatever it may be at the time, whereas, the exact opposite occurs when my head is full of rushing thoughts; such as, what to make for dinner, and getting on top of things so I'm ready to take her to school in the morning.

Making people feel heard is extremely important, especially as our lives seem to get busier and busier and – in part – this is what actively trusting and allowing your intuition to guide you does. If you listen, it can help you to pick up on the subtleties of the energy that surround a person. At any given time, you can learn, in the connective space between you, by altering your energy to blend with theirs. Thus, you both feel in a positive space when interacting with each other. It is a non-threatening space and this is why I use meditations in my workshops.

Meditations are important to help ground each person and to help them reconnect, after a break. It brings our energy back in and re-centres us for the afternoon session, which is where all the fun stuff takes place. This is when you can experience, for yourself, exactly what using your intuition feels like for you. This comes about after I show you how to use a few different tools to glean information. One that I often use is Psychometry, the reading of objects and the energy they hold. However, remember what I said. No two people will get the exact same information from the same object; and no answer they get is wrong, just different parts of the same.

Each person is then paired with a different partner for each new exercise, which shows you how this energy works with different people and for different people.

This is the part I really love. Everyone has so much fun watching the looks on each other's faces, as they realise that they've received innocent information about each other. Once could be a coincidence but three, four or five times makes them stop and think about what they are actually doing. They are using their intuition, reading energy and understanding how it feels to each of them. It is actually funny just how many *coincidences* there seem to be.

At the end of the day, we do another meditation to bring our energy back into the room and to close off within each person, before they leave. Food is a good re-balancer in these situations, so things such as tea and coffee, biscuits or small cakes are good to finish off the day. Yes, we get permission to eat that brownie or chocolate biscuit.

If you wanted an explanation about what exactly happens in these workshops, and why they are important, you would need to ask the people who participated. From where I am, it begins with people getting out of their own way. Most of us already believe in something greater than ourselves; outside of us. After that, it is not much of a stretch to believe there is also something greater within us. Something that knows we are so much more that what appears on our surfaces, and than what we show to the world...

*"One day something came along.
You began to accept that you,
all of you, had the answer.
The Gift of the Divine is within you.
It is there!*

*It has always been and always will be!
It is from you... it is for you... it is within you!
It is the gift you never see coming,
until you do!"*

*****

Meditation: Meditation takes many forms, and what may work for some, may not work for others. Meditation does not have to be the same thing for all people. Some sit down and close their eyes, which is what most people imagine when they hear the word meditation.

Think about the things you love to do. Some of these are a meditation in themselves. For instance, if you love bush walking, or just walking in your neighbourhood, that can be meditation. It may be that you love walking along the beach or swimming in the ocean, surfing or playing music. Some people chant, repeat a mantra, or hug a tree and listen to the wind speaking to them through the leaves.

You don't need to sit still. Moving meditations can be fantastic, because the movement takes you out of your mind. This allows you to still your busy thoughts. You can use anything you already do, where you feel time has slipped away, and where you may feel physically exhausted but your mind remains vibrant and clear.

The rejuvenation that you feel, mentally and spiritually, occurs because you're taken out of your conscious mind and away from your exhausting busy thoughts. It allows your subconscious mind to fill the space. Think of *meditation,* in any of its forms, as a mini-break, a weekend away from the stresses and demands of your day-to-day life.

In any event, when most people who don't meditate hear someone say, "You should try meditating," their first reaction is usually a deep sigh. Then they might say, "I don't have time for meditation, I'm too busy," or "I can't sit still for that long." I know that my first reaction to being told the exact same thing was something similar to this. What I've come to learn is that while you may think you have no time, the exact opposite is actually true. As Deepak Chopra says, "*The more you meditate the more time you find you have,*" (1998).

The purpose of meditation is to still the mind, so that you can connect with your soul. Your conscious thoughts can be going so fast you may feel as if you're on a merry-go-round, where the only way you can get off is letting the energy of its spinning throw you off. However, if you can sit still on the *horse* you're on, take a breath and merely witness what is going on around you without getting caught up in it, you will find you can enjoy being in that space for a while, and you can *relax* there.

When I first tried meditation, I tried different ones. I tried chanting, which didn't really work for me. I did a one-hour guided meditation, with others in a group, but I became fidgety after about ten minutes and then bored. I realised this was not the way to start my meditation practice. However, it did work for others. It may take you a while to discover which practice works for you.

After those failed experiments at meditation, I thought I can't do this meditation thing, and went back to doing the other things I loved doing. These were swimming in the ocean, walking and hugging trees. I know, *tree hugger* conjures up an image I'd rather you not have, now. What I mean by hugging trees is this. I loved walking, it was *my* place; the place where I felt strong, free and safe. I got the same feeling from being in the ocean. There is nowhere else I'd rather be, and I felt at home.

While I was out on my morning walk, along and around Avalon Beach, I noticed there were – and still are – some truly tall, beautiful Norfolk Island Palm Trees. These trees were planted like a border between the beach and playground and some lush grassy areas. One day I was feeling particularly fragile and I had no idea why, but it came into my head - intuition? – that I needed to go and hug a particular tree.

Of course, I felt silly. What would people think of me? But, I did it anyway. Why? Because I felt I would regret it if I didn't. I walked up to a tree that towered over me and checked to see if anyone was around then reached my arms around the tree trunk, so clumsily for the first time. Of course, I couldn't get them all the way around.

Then something magical happened. The more I relaxed into it the more comforted I felt. It felt as if I was being drawn into the tree itself and down into the earth where it was warm and safe. Then, thoughts came into my mind, just like in a reading but the thoughts themselves were different. These are the words that came and the words I will never forget.

"We were here, long before you came,
and we shall be here long after you have left.
We hold the earth strong for you,
just as we supply the air you breathe.
We have a symbiotic relationship, you and I . . ."

*****

I'm going to tell you about a meditation, probably the first one I ever ran myself. It was the night after a court case I mention later. There were to be four of us, but at the last minute one person had to pull out. Rather than have her miss out, I told her we were going to have her join in by phone, and I set a time for 08:00pm. My sister, Jane, and I sat down on the floor in my living room and called Tracey, who came onto the line straight away.

"I thought you'd never call," she said. I introduced Tracey to the other girls. Then I placed the phone on the floor with the open line, checking that Tracey could hear. I welcomed us into the meditation and stated our intention to clear and balance the day's energy, which we did. However, what came through to me was something completely unexpected, although welcome.

I said a blessing to protect our circle in love and the divine light and we began. Within five minutes – it could have been more as time disappears in the meditative state... saw her: a woman with blonde wavy hair and a long, white dress flowing around her.

She 'flew' to me so quickly that I could do nothing but watch her mesmerised by this, this... *angel*. She came to a stop directly in front of me. Nothing like this had ever happened to me before, but I didn't question the truth of it, not even to this day.

Then she spoke, answering my unspoken question, which was the same as when my father came to me, "I am here because of your kindness, for trying to help find me."

"But that was a month ago and I've heard nothing"

"I know and you won't personally, although you will in years to come."

"Where are you? Can I get someone to find you?"

"No. That is not why I am here. I came to let you know I have gone over. I am dead in your world."

Where are you, your body? At least I can help your family get closure."

"No Karen, this is a journey they must weather together. I have shown you where I was and how I got there but I will never be found. It is too late for that. They will look over every inch of the place and although they'll come close, they will never find me. She is gone. He will be caught and sentenced."

Then, she was gone. I opened my eyes and waited until everyone had finished. I closed off the mediation and the space.

"I'll go and make some tea for everyone, while you girls chat."

I got up and walked into the kitchen, still shaken and feeling so emotional. We had tea and some biscuits and then called it a night. Later, when I was in bed on my own, I sobbed at the futility of it all.

She was right! Many years later, I haphazardly picked up a magazine while waiting in line at the supermarket checkout. I chanced upon a small note in it, which confirmed to me that the family had received all the information I had sent.

*****

I've been doing meditations for a long time now and as far as meditation goes, I've tried many styles. However, I actually do have a manta that I love using any time I feel a little frazzled by life. I say it and I feel more able to function calmly, rather than allowing myself to get caught up in the craziness of life.

There are so many videos on the internet, and meditations by so many different people. I have certain ones I like and I choose what I want to meditate on each day. How long I need the mediation to be depends on how much time I have, especially in the morning. I like to save the longer ones for the evening, when I don't feel constrained by time. What these do for me is to take me to a place of supreme peace. It is the place where I connect with the core of who I am, my soul, and my essence. In the morning, and throughout my day, they help me to maintain a space of joy within.

CHAPTER 12

Finding your Purpose

Who would have thought that someone who had never been to a game of football – ever – would find out that a football club was the place where they would truly know without a doubt, what their life's purpose was! Thus it was for me, and it began like this.

I had been working part time in a friend's shop, when she called me, saying, "Hi Karen, I had a woman come into the shop this afternoon looking for a psychic. I thought you might be interested, so I told her I might have someone and that I would pass her number on. If you decide you're interested, give her a call."

I took down the number down and thanked my friend. It was only for one event, but the idea of working at the football club was interesting. I was intrigued to see how they thought it might work. I called the number and the woman set up a meeting at the club for the following Wednesday so I could meet the marketing manager.

I had never been to a football club. My son had played gridiron. We met at his office and discussed how he wanted this to work. After about half an hour, he suggested taking me to the ground so I could see the actual room I would be working in, to see if it would be all right. It was only a few minutes away.

After we arrived, he showed me up to the corporate boxes, and specifically the one I would be working in. I had a look around and decided I could make it work.

*****

"How does this *psychic thing* you do work?" he asked.

I knew he was interested, but not very confident that it was real.

"I could try to explain it to you, or if you'd like I can show you?" I offered.

"Oh, I don't know. I'm not sure I believe in that stuff."

"That's alright you don't have to. If you're worried, I don't do anything bad." I could see he wanted to, but was still hesitant; so I said, "Look, I can't and would never do anything without your permission, and I will stop straight away if you ask me to."

"Okay then, yes" he said.

"Good choice. It will be fun I promise."

After I finished the reading he looked at me strangely, something I'd become used to.

"How did you do that?" he asked.

I tried to explain how I did what I did. "First of all I must have your permission. I don't '*read*' anyone without their consent. The only time I may get something without it is if it was, say, a life and death situation. Thankfully, I haven't had one of those, yet."

"For a short time, I can *see* what is happening around you. I don't see everything because, well, that just sounds kind of creepy. But, it is not creepy or weird, although I will admit if you're not used to it, it can certainly seem that way. But, it really isn't. It isn't as if I have a clear picture of you and your life, only the bits and pieces your guides feel are relevant in this moment. Usually, it's nothing that makes any kind of sense to me anyway; only to you – hopefully! I don't need to know. Only that you understand and that it makes sense to you."

"It's also much easier to do for someone I don't know, because I can just open my energy up to accept what comes through. If I know the person, I have to block what I know through our relationship, friends, etc. first. Although, now that I've been doing this for a while, it doesn't seem matter if I know them or not."

We got up to go back to his office, where we talked about how it would work in the space and what usually happens on game days. We were walking through a row of seats. with him leading the way. when I blurted out "Do you know someone called William?"

He stopped so suddenly, I nearly bumped into him.

Without turning to me, he said, "Why?"

"There's is something about the relationship you have at the moment. Things will be changing in a few months and one of you is moving somehow. But they said not to worry you will be much happier in your new role."

He started walking again, although he didn't speak again until we got back to his office, where he told he wanted me for the event. As soon as he told me the date I realised I was already booked to do a psychic fair, so I had to decline.

*****

Early the following year, I received a call from a woman who had apparently taken over his role. She asked if I could make myself available for all of the home games for the upcoming season. Of course, I said yes. I was excited to try something new. On my first afternoon, before everyone started to arrive, the original man I'd met with came in to say hello.

It was a very interesting conversation. Apparently, what I had told him about last year had all come true, especially the part about William.

"That totally convinced me and got you the job," he said. I was thrilled it had worked out well for him. Then, the women who were booked in the booth started turning up, the game began and we all had a lot of fun.

Over the next ten years, I had a wonderful time doing readings for nearly everyone who came through our lounge: from media personalities, to sportsmen and women at the top of their game, as well as radio and TV presenters.

One afternoon, I was asked if I would join the guys in the radio room, to do a live reading before kick-off. I'd done a couple of radio gigs over the years and loved them. Once in the room, the energy picked up with the guys egging each other on to have a reading with me.

They all got into the *spirit of things* and before we went *live,* everyone in the room – including me – was laughing at the words I was saying and the fun and relaxed energy it brought into the room. However, my day here was mostly about making sure the women who were booked in to the lounge all received a reading from me, if they wanted one.

These women came from all over Sydney. They were people I would never have had a chance to meet under normal circumstances. I felt so grateful that I was able to help so many people in this way. Even some of the footballers, who were unable to play because of injury or whatever else, would come and visit the lounge. Sometimes their mates would dare one or two of them to sit down and have a reading with me.

All I can tell you is some were still laughing, although they were also curious, now. Others stopped laughing, and we did some good work together, with them asking how I knew this or that about them?

I would reply, "I don't know, not really it's an instinct thing. All I give you is what is I feel or hear and sometimes it's like a movie playing out in front of me. What I do know is that you were meant to get this from me today."

The time I spent at the football club, on game days, brought me such joy and a sense of helping others. It was truly a precious time for me. I was also not immune to having fun and I was even swept up into the electric energy of the family football day. We had a fantastic view of the field, although I very rarely got to watch the game, as I was so busy. The wins created an atmosphere that was indescribable and even I was known to get swept up in the singing as the team celebrated its victory with a lap around the field to thank the fans. I even met a woman I would later work with when I became a funeral director.

*****

One particular game, early in the season, comes to mind. At that stage, I had only been at the club for a couple of games. The woman, who was in charge of making sure things went smoothly in the box, was a huge football fan. She never asked me if I knew the outcome of a game before. Prediction is really not one of my things, or not one I concentrated on, anyway. Apparently, this was a big game and it was looking as if our team would lose, so, this time she did ask me. I will let her tell it in her words, then, I will tell you what I saw and heard.

'We were at a home game and our team were losing. It was very tense in the lounge. I was really anxious as I'm a huge football fan. Things were not looking good at all – we were losing by 12 points with only 20 minutes to go. I looked across the room and there was Karen watching the game, all calm. I caught her eye with a pleading look in mine. I had never dared to ask straight out 'are we going to win today?!' This time I just wanted to be put out of my misery. Karen looked at me and mouthed 'It's okay... relax... just keep watching'... and I did and I kid you not, it's like a new team developed on the field and our team went on to win by 2 points.'

M. F.

As soon as she asked me, an old movie that I loved popped into my head. It was called '*Angels in the Outfield*' (1994). As soon as I saw it, I knew our team was going to win, and I nodded to her. There were only twenty minutes to go before full time, and it was explained to me, later, that we needed three converted tries to win. The other team was playing extremely well and we seemed to have run out of energy. The other team were all over us, and winning seemed impossible. After a few minutes, she looked over again. I mouthed '*It's okay... relax... just keep watching*', but she still looked doubtful. I know it seems strange, but when you trust your intuition and the information you're being given you just *know truth when you see it, when you feel it, or hear it* and being calm is easy.

I could see the game being played out in my mind, and there were *angels* all over the field. Suddenly, our team changed completely and started to come back with a rush of new energy. They scored and converted their last try in the last minute of the game, to win by two points.

I also *knew* that we were going on to win the Grand Final that year, not that I told anyone. At least not until the day when my girlfriend and I were sitting in the stands with fabulous seats and watching it play out in real life.

Of course, she was saying..." you know don't you? No, don't tell me! I don't want to know... tell me! I can't stand it."

"I'm not going to spoil the game for you. All I will tell you is that there is a four in the score. Now don't ask me anymore. Let's just have fun and watch the game."

She looked at me fluctuating between certainty and doubt. It made for an interesting game I can tell you. In addition, it was my first Grand Final and I was as excited as any child, or football lover, could be, especially when a Black Hawk helicopter landed in the middle of the field. Talk about a surreal moment.

I don't like predictions. One, people probably wouldn't believe you. Two, if they do believe you it would ruin the game or whatever it is in their life that is important to them at that time. In addition, there is always a possibility that something will change, and the outcome that I saw for them won't happen. It sounds as if I'm hedging my bets doesn't it? However, it is all about energy. With so many people's energy involved, something can always change. Yet, in that moment standing there, I was being shown so much light around the players and all over the field that I knew a win was assured.

This story is a really great example of how we can use our intuition, gut instinct, or whatever tools you have at your disposal to create the life you want. The *dream*, or the *wish* is only a part of it. Of course this is not only about energy helping the players. It starts with the players themselves; the unique talent of each player and the combined talent of all the players on the field. If their wish to win is to become their reality, they must all focus on their combined goal and must not allow anything else into their energy. This was their year. They all knew it, and they acted and played accordingly.

Anytime anyone is filled with knowledge of their purpose, and all they can and want to do to focus on their passion and purpose; and then, all their energy helps move them towards achieving that goal. When they take action, and do what they know they must do to make their dream happen, when they share their gift and make it a reality, there can be no other outcome. Not for them, not for me, and not for you.

Oh, did I mention the name of the lounge we were in? It was called the '*Wings*' Lounge.

*****

Working in the club also taught me a lot about my boundaries and how my energy works during short, back-to-back readings. I also have a time limit where my energy can start to fade. Seeing so many people, for such a concentrated stretch of time, is as depleting for me as it is exhilarating. It is also dependent upon the energy of the people I see. Over the years in the club, I learnt how to balance my energy and how to set my boundaries so that I didn't take on other energies around me.

During my time there, I also came to truly understand and appreciate why my emotions and feelings were being tapped into, as I read for people. For as long as I can remember, I've always been able to feel other people's emotions. I always thought this was because of my Libran nature. For example, I can always see both sides of an argument, and can give credence to both parties involved.

When I was growing up, I wondered if this was in fact a gift, because I always found myself in the role of a peacemaker. More often than not, that left me feeling on the outside of things in the long term. As I got older, and after I had begun to accept my psychic abilities, I realised that many of these extra feelings I was having, were actually connected to my intuitive and psychic abilities.

I never had a word for it. I just felt it. Then one day, I can't even remember when it was, I read a short article about empaths. At last, I understood that I was an empath, with psychic abilities or vice versa.

I really don't think it's important how one is described, only that you have the tools at your disposal to be able to help other human beings, and yourself for that matter. My life and my over abundance of feelings finally made sense. A lot of us are empathic, in some way, without ever putting that word to it.

To explain: We all know the words *sympathy* and *empathy*. The meaning of these words, as shown in the Collins Dictionary, is this. Empathy. "the ability to share another person's feelings and emotions as if they were your own." Sympathy is when "you are sorry for them."

I believe that the difference between these words is that to feel empathy for someone means you've also experienced the same or very similar feelings yourself, so you have *firsthand* knowledge of exactly how they are feeling. Whereas when you feel sympathy for someone, you're able to *imagine* how they might be feeling, although it also seems to resonate with *pity*. People may need your help – at some point in all our lives we all do – but, for me personally, *pity* seems a rather demeaning word and a little judgemental. But, that's how I feel about it.

*"Feelings
are everywhere.
Be gentle."*

Anonymous

*****

I did get some private jobs, from some of the women who came into the lounge. One was for a girls' night in with an Arabian Nights theme. This was lots of fun. All the girls were in a great mood and having fun, and so the readings were fun to do.

There was one particular group that I still remember. They were a group of girls, who worked together in admin. They wanted me to go to their place of work after they closed, because they lived in different places and it was easier this way. We settled on a date and I explained I would only be able to give five readings of half an hour each.

The night was going well and the first three girls were extremely happy with their readings. Then, the fourth girl came in. She sat down across from me and the reading began.

At one point I said, "Oh, you're going on a holiday, for two weeks to the snow. That will be fun."

"No I don't have any holidays planned at the moment," she replied. "I've always wanted to go to the snow, but it's so expensive I doubt I'll get there."

"Are you sure?" I asked. "I definitely see you away in the snow."

She couldn't make sense of it and neither could I, because it was there for her.

"Oh well I don't know what to tell you." So apart from that, she was happy with the rest of her reading. She left and sent the final girl in.

Her reading went well, and she was happy and confirmed everything I was saying to her. The girls outside were getting louder and laughing a lot. Luckily, we were finishing up as their laughter was becoming too loud for me to *hear* anything else. Five minutes later, we both walked out to join them. The girl who I'd seen just before was laughing and so were all the others.

"You will never guess what happened?" she said to me. "When I came out, my husband called. He just rang me to say he's booked a holiday for two weeks in the snow for my birthday!!!"

I was as shocked as she was and we all started laughing so hard it hurt. Talk about right on cue! These are the times I really love what I do: when people can get so much joy out of it.

"Everything you want is only a thought away."

CHAPTER 13

Taking the Leap

The idea for this book came to me five years ago. I was off work for a week, because I had hurt my leg and was unable to walk. I don't know if it was my leg, or being stuck at home *relaxing*, but I also ended up with the flu, which miraculously disappeared after I went back to work, the following week. Anyway the point is I was home. I was feeling sorry for myself and I was bored.

I was lying on the lounge one day, when this idea popped into my head. Quite literally, the words 'Road Trip with a Psychic' were in my head and they would not go away. This is what happens when spirit is trying to get my attention, and wants me to write it down. Sometimes I don't, for whatever reason; I'm tired, I want to keep on sleeping, or whatever. But if I don't write it down, spirit has other ideas and will just keep repeating the same phrase over and over in my head like a broken record until I do write it down.

Sometimes it can be for ten minutes or more, if I've been asleep. It is like someone pulling on my arm trying to get me to wake up (my gorgeous little granddaughter comes to mind here) but all I want to do is sleep. Sleep never wins (nor with my granddaughter either), although once I do start to write the words down, they will keep flowing faster than my hand can write them or sometimes they just stop. That day they stopped.

I thought about the phrase for a while and it intrigued me. What did it actually mean to me? I thought about the question in different ways and then the idea began to form fully, and the *goose bump* thing happened. My whole body was freezing, showing me that this idea in my head was an absolute truth for me. I was so happy I could have jumped up and down on the couch If only I could have moved my leg. The pen was back in my hand and I started writing.

I actually felt grateful that I'd hurt my leg, otherwise I would not have been lying on the lounge at home with the time and the space to write, after this exciting thought had got me back into writing again.

I started to write. By then, I was four days into my week off and by the end of the week at home I had three short stories. That appeared to be the end of that!

Over the few years since then, those stories kept popping into my head every so often. I would think about them for a little while, and take them out for a read. However, so much was going on in my life, there was never any time for me, let alone throwing writing into the mix so I'd put them away again. At least that's what I kept telling myself. But writing would not let me be, and every so often some words or a phrase would come and I would feel compelled to write them down. I always felt as if I would miss something important, something special, if I just let them go. I actually tested this theory out once, without realising that was what I was doing.

I'm not quite sure when it was. However, I must have been in a very deep sleep at the time. I remember a phrase continually making its way into my conscious mind, but I felt so tired that I simply couldn't move to get what I needed to write it down. I made the mistake of allowing it to go on and I began listening as the words kept rolling out one after the other. By the time, I got to around the third or fourth sentence I woke up in a panic and raced to grab a pen and paper.

I kept writing, while struggling to find fragments of the sentences, I'd let fall away. No luck, only bits and pieces remained that I could make no coherent sentence out of. I was so annoyed with myself that I never did that again. Obviously, it would continue without me transcribing. Mostly these words felt as if teachings, memories from a time long gone by or thoughts were given through me. I don't know which of these sources they were, but it didn't seem to matter, as long as they were out of my head and held somewhere, to revisit on another day.

*****

Then came 2020. What a crazy year! I hurt my leg again in mid-March and I ended up with the flu halfway through the year. I was so sick with the flu; all I could do was sleep. I'm talking twenty-nine hours solid; the first time my head hit the pillow.

When I wasn't sleeping, thoughts of writing a book from my short stories started to filter through my mind again, but I was so sick I couldn't do anything but go back to sleep. Covid-19 made it crucial to stay at home, whenever possible.

This was extremely isolating, especially as I was cut off from my family, as I'm sure many of you know too well. Eventually, after two Covid-19 tests both proving it had 'just' been the flu, I made it back to work, and all thoughts of writing flew out the window again, along with the flu.

Then about a month later, and after making sure I was completely healthy, I decided to go visit a girlfriend who had broken her ankle. On the way, I noticed our local Sunday market was on, behind Pittwater RSL Club. Even although I'd driven right past it, I suddenly thought "I should go in and buy some organic fruit for her." I found somewhere to park, and then walked back and began wandering through the marketplace.

I walked past stall after stall, before finding the fruit and vegetables. I paid for my purchases and decided to wander around a bit, social distancing of course, with a mask, gloves, and all. I hadn't really been out for what felt as if an eternity to me. It was fun looking at all the different things.

I was about to walk past a stall that seemed to have a bit of everything for children. As I did, something knocked the side of my leg. I turned to see what it was. My skirt twisted in something and nearly pulled it off the table. I grabbed at it so it didn't fall. It turned out to be a book. I looked at it for a moment and the cover drew me in.

It was mostly in black and white, and featured a woman wearing a big, red rose on a ring on her hand. Oh my gosh! I recognised the woman on the cover. I realised it was a woman I had heard speaking at the first writer's workshop from Hay House, in Melbourne eleven years ago. Yes, I know I've a really good memory.

There were great speakers that day and I had heard most of them speak at other venues over the years. However for some reason I remembered this woman's story and her words "If I can do it, you can do it" and they had stayed with me. I talk about 'signs' all the time. Sometimes they are very subtle and other times they are, full on in-your-face kinds of sign. Well this book falling off the table and into my hands was a huge *in-my-face one* for me. I had to have that book. I mean it had practically said, "Take me home with you."

As I've often said before, when you're open to the signs around you, recognising them becomes so much easier. Especially once you come to understand what each sign means to you and your specific understanding of them. This was not one of those signs I had to think about to understand its meaning. This was so clear, it was practically screaming at me to stop procrastinating and get on with it.

However, I'd only come in to get some fruit and I had no money left. All I had was my card. How could I buy a book for $1 on my card? While I was thinking what I could do, I heard a voice behind me that I recognised. My granddaughter was there with her other nanny.

I turned and said, "Hi! How funny bumping into you here!" As my granddaughter and I hugged each other I asked her other nanny "Could I borrow a $1? I haven't got any change, and I need to get this book. I'll pay you back, I promise."

She didn't hesitate and I bought the book feeling guilty, but not enough to let it go. Who knows how long it had been trying to find me, before it ended up on that table waiting for me. I also discovered that the book had been signed by the author. Even although it wasn't addressed to me, I knew with absolute certainty it was meant to come to me.

I kissed my granddaughter on her head, and they went on their way. I headed back to my car and on to the hospital.

That night, and over the next few days, every time I had a spare minute, I read the book. One night, I looked at the back of the book and noticed the author contact details. I went to her website and found that she also did mentoring. Without actually knowing what I was hoping for I blindly sent an email, asking about mentoring. I've never emailed any of the authors I've read, until that night and I've read heaps.

The next day I was at work. Just after finishing time, as I was gathering my things to leave, my phone rang. It was Rachael, the author of the book. I was astounded that she had actually called me. I wasn't really expecting a reply to my email. We seemed to hit it off straight away.

Now, its four weeks later and I'm totally invested in creating a book from my three short stories and more importantly finishing it. For me the value of a book is in what it means to the person reading it. Some books are priceless and this one was to me. It took me from procrastination and moved me right into action. Oh, and I also paid back the money I borrowed, to buy it.

If I hadn't gone with what my intuition was so obviously trying to tell me, I know I would not be writing this now. Our intuition is a powerful guide. It guides us towards our best path. Sometimes we listen, sometimes we don't. I could have shrugged off the feeling to stop at the markets that day, and kept right on going. However, I also believe that timing is important. Five years ago, I wasn't ready to write my book, but now, everything just fell together, like Dominoes.

One thing leads to another, and to another, etc. I also believe that when you're on track with whatever your purpose is, things happen with ease. You move into the flow of your life, and no force is involved. Only action can move it, now. It's about timing and listening to your intuition! These two things will give you a reason, but taking action on them is what keeps you going forward in your life.

Was this why I felt so compelled to hop on a plane to Melbourne, eleven years ago, to attend a workshop? Was it because, even although I didn't know it then, I was subconsciously making a memory that I would needed at some point in the future to guide me in the direction of my heart's longing? Was this why I felt so compelled to go into the markets that day? Was it because, at a deep-soul level, I needed to call up that memory, because the timing was right now, for me to write? It's a bit of a riddle, isn't it? It's one that I find interesting and fun to ponder.

Would I have bought the book at the markets if I hadn't gone to that workshop and heard Rachael speaking? I don't think so. It would not have triggered a memory, because I would not have been there to have that memory created. The memory I needed in order to buy the book that led me to write the email that led me to begin writing my book. As I said, Dominoes!

"One falls and knocks its brother;
a chain reaction set in place.
As movement follows movement,
all leading to a space.

The answer still unclear,
until the wrapping falls.
The gift is seen, is heard
No barriers… No more walls!

It sparks a conversation,
What ride is this we're on?
With unclear destination,
Where all challenges are gone.

No more hesitation
as acknowledgement ignites
a brand new conversation...
Until we get it right!"

*****

This is not the end, only the beginning. It is also the year of Covid-19 and that in itself presents many challenges. The continued isolation, especially through Christmas, didn't help with my depression. Sometimes, it took a lot for me to get up to write, even though I know that when I'm actually writing I feel better, happier, and excited. This is especially true, when the words flow, and time totally disappears. I even forget to eat, and that's saying something!

Some days even twelve hours sleep doesn't seem enough. It's hard to try to convince myself, that if I can just get up, start moving and sit down at my computer, I know that – despite whatever I am or am not feeling... I can be productive, doing something I love. This is how I got myself through lockdown, until it ended and I could see my family again.

I also understand that I'm in the company of so many other Australians, and so many others all across our big, beautiful world. We are all going through the same things. However one of the good things to come out of this is learning. If we didn't realise it before, we now understand how very important family is. When things are not going well, it is your family and friends, and their love and support that get us through the times, when we need a bit more than we can give ourselves.

"Our anxiety does not come from thinking about the future, but from wanting to control it."

Kahlil Gibran

CHAPTER 14

Mum and the Final Lesson

It is really hard to write this today. Mum passed over eighteen months ago, and it is still very fresh. I miss her more than I thought possible. I went to call Mum again today. I can't tell you how many times this has happened over these past months. I still go to pick up the phone, to call her, and catch myself. At other times, I might hear something funny or a story I know mum would like. I think "I must tell Mum about this!"

Mum and her brother, who died four months after her and another uncle who also died not long after were the last of their generation. It is a surreal feeling that each of us must experience at some point. Knowing you and your siblings are the head of your family or families now. There is no one above you except for all of those high above you.

When the realisation of Mum's death hits me, I feel emptiness like a deep, deep well in my heart. Sometimes the crying drowns me and then at other times I feel a melancholy sadness that distracts me from daily life. Mum taught me many things during our life together, but in her last ten years I taught her things and told her things that she was ready to listen to, and – now... felt she was really listening. This was because of what happened on the day of an operation mum needed to have, well over twelve years ago.

We found out that Mum needed a double by-pass. Two of the main arteries to her heart were blocked, so Mum was booked to have her operation as soon as possible. She was eighty years of age, and we were all worried.

The night before her operation, we were allowed to visit for a short while. Mum was very agitated, saying that she had to make sure her will was in order. After a while, and after some convincing that her will, was fine she finally relaxed. I don't mind telling you she had me a little rattled with all the will talk. Once she had settled my daughter and I kissed her and left. My brother was going to the hospital to see Mum in the morning, before her surgery and she had spoken with my sister while I was there, so we knew mum was okay.

Mum's surgery had been booked for 07:00am in the morning. At that time, I was driving down Mona Vale Road on my way to work... it was normally bumper to bumper with cars, but there were very few on the road this morning which was odd. I don't know exactly what time it was but one moment I was driving, and the next there was a kind of window or screen right in front of me. The car windscreen had disappeared and I was watching mum's surgery.

I saw a man standing at the end of the operating table, holding his hand out to her. It was Brian, the love of her life, who had departed ten years before. Mum had sat up on the table and was reaching for him.

I screamed "Noooo! Mum! I'm not ready." I watched my mother lie back down into her body on the operating table. All of a sudden, I saw I was still driving along Mona Vale Road on my way to work In St Ives.

I was shaking and my breathing deep and quick. What had I just seen? Even for me, this was weird and I had not experienced anything like it before. You may also ask if this really happened, and what happened to the car?

From everything that I've learnt, along my crazy road trip, I believe that time bends, somehow folding back in on itself. So, in this instance, I had somehow stepped out of linear time and into a space where all time happens simultaneously. This created a way for me to be where I truly wanted to be in that moment, in that nanosecond.

While at the same time sitting in my car, driving to work and wishing the day would fly so I could get to the hospital to see Mum, I knew that she was alright and had come through her surgery because I had actually been there with her.

Did my thoughts create this? Was it the power of my love for her and the thought of losing Mum so soon? Or am I crazy? You tell me. All I can tell you is that what I saw and what I knew was absolutely true for me. I did also call the hospital a couple of hours later, to be told that Mum had come out of her surgery and was in recovery, where she would stay for a while. I also found out later that Mum's operation had actually been taking place at the same time I was seeing it.

Later that afternoon, as I was driving over to the hospital, I thought about what had happened to me that day. How could I possibly think, even for a moment, that I had the power to prevent someone else leaving this life, unless they chose to do so? How egotistical was I? Of course I couldn't.

Mum had come out of recovery and was sitting up in bed two days later, doing much better. When I arrived to see her, I discovered something that was an even bigger shock for me, than for Mum herself. I walked in and sat down beside her bed.

"Hi Mum, how are you feeling?" I asked.

"I'm okay," she replied.

She seemed a bit odd to me. "Are you sure you're okay?"

"Yes but I have to tell you something. You're the only person I can tell, Karen."

"Okay Mum I'm listening, what's wrong?"

"There's nothing wrong, but I have to tell you what happened." I died in that operation. I could hear them all talking about me."

"What do you mean you died Mum?"

"I died while they were operating on me. I heard the doctor say 'It's too late she's gone.' But, the nurse told him the pacemaker has just kicked back in so he kept trying to get me back. Karen, I saw God!"

I remembered my vision of her from my car, and what she was telling me started to freak me out.

"How do you know you saw God, Mum?"

"Because he was standing at the end of the bed and I was getting up to go. Karen, you're the only person I know who would believe me, but you can't tell anyone else. They'll think I'm crazy."

"I know you're not crazy, Mum. I love you. You just need to get some rest now so you can come home soon."

I never did tell anyone, until now, and I know she wouldn't mind. I didn't tell Mum about my vision that same day, either. I was full of guilt, even though I know it wasn't my fault.

Mum was a bit like me, well, how I used to be. I always needed proof for myself and then I believed. Although at the time of her passing, she taught me to trust what I know and never to doubt myself or what I do, again.

This was the final lesson Mum taught me, and she left me in no doubt to the truth of it. It was the most important gift she had ever given me and it came on the day she died.

It had been an emotional couple of weeks for me, for both of us. I lived with Mum for the last two years of her life, through loving hugs, angry outbursts and falling over in fits of laughter, me that is, not Mum. She might have broken a hip, "and we'd be up the creek without a paddle" as she used to say. The kind of close bond Mum and I shared during her last years, and especially her last six months, was another gift for me. As Mum's dementia became worse, we knuckled down together doing what needed to be done. First, so she could stay at home as long as was possible and second to help her keep her dignity, so that she was still able to keep her funny playful, personality, when she chose to of course.

The strength of her personality began to fade the more fragile she became physically. Although as the dementia got worse, more stories came up about her life and they showed what a strong woman she had been physically, from a young age. It was heartbreaking for me to watch her slowly disappearing day by day, and hour by hour. We had to get through some extremely difficult times together, but we managed our roles with grace and ease.

After Mum's death I seemed to breeze through it all, full of composure; from arranging her funeral, the eulogy I gave and the wake that followed. I put this down to the years I spent as a funeral director. It felt normal arranging this and, unlike my father, I've never seen Mum, well her spirit, since the day she passed.

"I know you're out there somewhere Mum, 'living' your death until you decide if you want to come back and do it all over again or not!"

****

I'm positive your day is more active than mine is today. Today I got up with nothing to do, so scary and I was a little apprehensive. Then my thoughts started drawing me into the past.

I found my thoughts somewhat disconcerting, although now I've the value of hindsight to draw from about it. All I can do today is sit on the balcony of Mum's unit. Inertia has taken my mind back 35 years ago, to June/July 1984.

I find myself sitting on this same balcony having the same thoughts as I had then. Where do I go from here? What do I do with my life? The questions and my life seemed a little less daunting back then. I still felt like a *girl* who had her whole life ahead of her. Now, it feels very different to be sitting here, again, and still asking these same questions.

If life could give me a handbook, it could not be any better. Talk about coming full circle. My gosh! With so much life in between, I still managed to end up sitting on my mother's balcony asking, "Where do I go from here?"

I'm not depressed, if that is how it sounds. It is an observation that I find ironic. It's just the end of life as I know it, and with so much of life now behind me, I feel this is the last chapter for me. So, I want to make it an extraordinary one!

Some days I feel like Rip Van Winkle, waking up after a long, long sleep. The difference is where he couldn't remember, I can't forget. I can remember all of where my life went, including the twists and turns, and the miles and miles of dragging everything with me, uphill, ironically like 'Jack and Jill'. Most of the time I was making life harder than it had to be. But, that would have meant listening to my intuition, every time it tried to get my attention, over the years, and of course I didn't do that in the beginning.

As I've said, I'm just like you. Sometimes we let our emotions get the better of us, when maybe we shouldn't. I'm here – not so much exhausted from my stuff, because I'm happy with the choices I've made, and with a little help from the *other side* – but emotionally exhausted from the weeks, and maybe months I spent of cleaning and clearing out 35 years of Mum's life and getting her home ready for sale.

Yes, Mum passed over. Dementia and death finally took her to a place where she would be free of her tiny, fragile body. She is free to be her best self, with nothing to keep her bound to bed or her beloved balcony.

Although I swear, five days before she left this earth, I felt her come back to the balcony and the home she adored one last time to say goodbye.

I was sitting on her balcony. It was the middle of Monday afternoon. I had been up and down a few times to get a cup of tea, food etc. Mum had left for hospital and then 'The Resort', as we called the RSL Life Care, The War Veterans where Mum went to live straight after hospital, ten weeks before.

The first time I passed her bedroom door I noticed it was slightly ajar, which was odd since I had closed her bedroom door, and only went into her room to clean. I couldn't face walking past and seeing her not there.

I closed her door again, not thinking too much about it. Next time I got up to go to the kitchen for a cuppa (I love tea, all kinds), her door was open again. 'Weird" I thought. I got my tea, closed her door, and sat back on the balcony. The third time this happened, I knew there was no wind. I knew I had closed it.

This time I left it wide open and said aloud "Okay Mum come on through." I could actually feel Mum moving through the unit. I realised she was taking one last look at the home she loved, before she left.

Sometimes the bond is so strong, our loved ones don't want to or can't move on while we're with them, and sometimes they can. The bond mum and I shared had certainly grown very strong over the past couple of years, as dementia took up more and more residence in Mum's mind and it became harder watching this happen.

Maybe Mum needed to create some distance until she was ready to move on. I just wish she had thought of a less painful way, for me at least.

I'd got shingles a week-and-a-half before, and was unable to see Mum until the next Thursday. We still spoke on the phone, but it wasn't the same.

Seeing Mum in such a vulnerable state broke my heart. Being able to comfort her and give her the respect we all deserve helped comfort me. Two nights after Mum's 'visit' home, I received a call from Mum's nurse.

I had just been cleared by my doctor and was able to go back to work the next day, so I told her I was coming in the following morning to see Mum before work.

She stopped me and said, "Karen, your mum is not good. I think you need to call the family tonight."

All the air in my lungs seemed to rush out, as I took in what she was actually saying.

"I, um... I'll call them now. I'll be there as soon as I can. Thank you so much for letting me know."

I called my daughter straight away.

"Mum's nurse just called. Nana is not well and she told me to call the family. Can you go straight there, now! I don't want her to be alone."

"I'm on my way Mum."

"Thanks love, I'll be there as fast as I can. I'm throwing some things in a bag now and calling your uncle. I love you. I'm on my way honey. I could hear her crying, but knew we'd be together soon."

I dialled my brother's number as I raced down the stairs. He lived a few hours away.

I told him "The nurse just called and told me to call the family. They know it won't be long now. I'm heading over and your niece should already be with her. I'm not trying to scare you, but her nurse has always been really up front with me so you need to know."

I could hear his thoughts were a jumbled mess like mine.

"I'm coming down first thing in the morning."

"Okay I'll see you then."

I was on the road five minutes later. My foot wanted to hit the accelerator as hard as It could go but that was my need taking over. I knew that at this time of night I would be there in forty-five minutes, catching all the lights and sticking to the speed limit. Somehow, I just focused on the road ahead, trying to keep panic at bay.

About ten minutes into my trip, my brother called me back and said that they were also coming down and would be there in about two hours.

"Okay, please be safe and don't do anything crazy."

"I promise I won't. See you soon, Sis."

He hung up and I concentrated on getting to Mum and my daughter, but I couldn't forget the call. The call you never want to get. When I arrived at Mum's room, her breathing was laboured and there are three nurses with her. My daughter was sitting staring vacantly at the TV while they did their work.

Mum's life had been longer than most, but this was my mother, so my heart broke the minute I received that call. My daughter and I sat and talked. My brother and sister-in-law arrived two hours later. Mum had been sleeping since we arrived, so I updated them on what the nurses had told me. Mum had been on oxygen since Sunday evening. It was now Wednesday night. She needed it to help her breath. After a few minutes, my daughter left and I walked her out to the car to give my brother some time alone with his Mum.

While I was out, I called our sister to let her know and asked her to come down. She said she was already coming down and would come straight to us from the airport the following night, which she did.

After my brother left, the nurses set up a mattress for me on the floor, so I could be close to Mum. It didn't take long for me to fall asleep. I must have been dreaming, because I could hear someone faintly, calling out to me in the background, but not enough to wake me. A moment later I jumped and then sat up as the screaming in my ear became coherent.

"UNFORGETTABLE! UNFORGETTABLE!"

It took a few seconds for it to sink in my foggy brain.

"Unforgettable?" Oh my God! Brian, is that you?"

The screaming stopped. I knew what I had to do. I looked over at Mum and she appeared to be sound asleep, but her hands were raised above her and it looked as if she was grabbing at something. I pulled a chair over to her bedside, and found what I was looking for on my phone.

For the next hour I played the song that had been *their song,* Unforgettable, by Nat King Cole over and over again, beside Mum's ear until she settled. Then, I turned it off and went back to bed remembering what Brian had told me after he had passed away, twenty-three years before.

*****

Mum struggled with Brian's death. He was the love of her life. His passing had been sudden and a shock to all of us who loved him, but it hit Mum especially hard. Brian came to me a few weeks *after* his passing and said:

"Tell her I will be back for her when she is ready, but that will not be for about twenty of your years."

I promised him and then he left. I told Mum this at the time and said that I truly believed what he had said to me with all of my heart. Mum appeared to take some comfort in this, and she learned how to go on without him.

*****

The next night it happened again. I awoke to some strange sounds. I turned over to see Mum was almost out of bed. She had one foot on the floor and her arms were outstretched again. I jumped out of bed to help Mum back into bed, half-lying half-sitting. For someone so tiny and frail, she was so heavy.

One of the nurses opened the door just at that same moment and together we helped get Mum into a more comfortable position. Then the nurse left. I got out my phone and sat down again with Mum and played *their song* over and over again, until I could feel that Mum was more settled. Then, I went then back to sleep myself. That was about four am.

I awoke again about two hours later, with an urgent feeling. I had to have a shower, and to get to work – just to check in – and would call the nurses in a couple of hours to see how Mum was doing. In hindsight, it was the wrong choice for me, for what I wanted. But I believe it was the right choice, the perfect choice, for what my Mum wanted. Looking back it is obvious to me that she had one more lesson she wanted to impress upon me, painful as it was at the time.

At 09:50am, I got a strong feeling that I needed to call the nurses. Before, I could pick up the phone they called me and said it wouldn't be long now and that I should come right away. My daughter and I spoke only for long enough to know we were both heading over to Mum's. It quite literally took ten minutes to get there and park and by then the manager, Rochelle was taking my arm in hers, as she walked me around to Mum's room.

"It is very near and we may not make it, Karen. I just want you to be prepared." I started walking quickly. If I'd been on my own, I would have run as fast as I could, but this too was not to be.

We got to Mum's room and stepped inside. Mum was behind the door. Rochelle stopped. I could feel the strength of her arm imperceptibly holding mine. I heard her voice and the nurse who was with Mum said something.

Rochelle turned to me and said, "Karen, I'm sorry she's just left us."

I moved past her and went straight to my mother. One look and I knew what they told me was true. "Oh Mum," my head fell down beside her and my arms wrapped around her. My tears flowed as silently as she'd slipped away from me, from all of us.

I heard a door across the courtyard, and I knew my daughter was coming. I couldn't let her into the room without knowing Mum had already gone. Rochelle asked if she could make Mum more comfortable (my funeral director training kicked in).

"Yes of course please do what you need to. I have to get to my daughter before she comes in to let her know," I answered.

I walked out. She looked at me, her eyes filled with hope.

"We didn't make it sweetheart."

We held each other in our sorrow, and then walked inside to sit with Mum and Nana, We talked and remembered her the way only we two could. Rochelle and all of the nurses were our angels that day.

They made sure we had something to drink and eat as we said our own private farewells, knowing our lives would never feel the same again. We sat there for two hours, talking, crying, and remembering the love and laughter – mostly the laughter – she had brought to our lives.

I stayed with Mum, for a while longer, after my daughter had left to pick up her daughter from preschool. I stayed until I could find enough strength to walk away, not really comprehending just how different my life would be without her, from here onwards. After saying goodbye to the women, the *angels* who had helped Mum and us, I got into my car and drove to a nearby local car park.

I knew how important time was, over these next couple of hours, to arrange Mum's service for my family.

Mum's family had to have enough time to book flights, so that all could attend. I put on my funeral director's hat, figuratively speaking, and within one hour, I'd managed to arrange and book in dates, times and everything else needed for Mum's service. I made two quick calls to my brother and sister, to let them know, so everyone could make their plans etc.

I took off my 'hat' and tried to contain my grief on my drive home. I thought about this last lesson that Mum had made sure she taught me, as she left. For years, I've been telling clients that death is just another doorway, but one that we cannot open, until it is our time to do so. I say that the people we love, who have passed away, are only behind a door, which we cannot go through, yet.

They can hear you, from behind this *door*. They can see you and they can help you, if you trust what your intuition is telling you. That was my lesson. Mum was making absolutely sure that I knew it to be true. Knowing Mum as I did…as I do, she gave me this last gift to help free me from any doubt – no matter how small – about myself and what I do.

The things I know to be true about death are: The body dies but the spirit, our soul, the essence of who we are never dies. It moves on to re-join its soul family, or in my Mum's case to join her one true love, who kept his promise and came back for her. Their souls and all the other free souls are in heaven, in the ethers, and are eternal.

The ego is the gatekeeper of our own creation to stop us from trusting, believing and – more importantly from knowing that we can choose to create a better life for ourselves and a less fear-filled death.

Fear is a construct built by the ego. Fear is a perception. Fear it is not real. We can choose fear or we can choose to embrace knowing that we are the creators of our physical life and we are the creators of the way we leave this physical life. What I know for sure is that both my parents were welcomed by friends and people who loved them. Death was not their enemy. Death was their freedom. The thoughts and feelings we create around the about the death process can hinder our acceptance of it. If we accept this as a truth, of what need we be fearful? Death is the beginning, the re-birthing of an entirely new existence and experience.

"Fear is not a stumbling block.
It is a springboard,
to living a more luscious life."

CHAPTER 15

Looking for Signs

Do you believe in signs? I do. Often, *signs* appear to help guide us in all areas of our life, but all too often we miss them. Sometimes we may be moving too quickly to recognise them for what they are. Other times we may actually understand what they mean but choose to ignore them. The thing is, these *signs* never go away. They linger until the time when we want to know, when we want to understand their meaning rather than running from them.

Mostly we either choose to ignore them, or we embrace them completely, as I've done and as many, many more do I'm sure. Whatever our reasons for acting one way or the other, our intuition never gives up. It never stops trying to help guide us in the direction of our best life possible.

When someone we love dies, all we want is a message that they are all right and that they are happy. So, now is a good time to learn what your signs are, because they will use these to get your attention, any way they can, if they have a message for you. This is a natural part of life and death, too. Work on learning what they are for you and on trusting your intuition, that the signs you get are not just a coincidence, but are as real as the love you have.

Just ask and they will answer. At first, it might seem cryptic, but once you learn the language of your signs, it will be a language you will love. It will also bring you so much fulfilment.

The following is a short note that came through from my Dad, only a couple of months after Mum passed over. I had been thinking of her and, without putting any real thought to what I was saying, I said aloud "Dad, is Mum okay?" The following is what he said to me:

"Oh there was a big party when your mum, her brother, and my younger brother arrived I can't tell you! All is forgiven here and we were all 'Dancing on the Ceiling' or so the song goes. My sister is fine. She is sooo happy to have both her brothers back again. It is very different here. Everyone knows and understands everything... 'here' is only love sweetheart."

*****

Now, before we begin, I would like to share another experience with you, one I had this Christmas past. It was the second Christmas since Mum had passed over, and I was with my daughter and granddaughter for dinner on Christmas Eve, but I was really missing Mum; especially, when we sat down to eat and I saw a photo of Mum had been put on the table to include her.

I was back again in the morning to open presents and to have Christmas breakfast together.

"Quick Mum, come here," my daughter said. I hurried into the kitchen to see two white cockatoos sitting on the windowsill. That white cockatoo was my sign that Mum was near, was here. Straight away, I knew in my heart that it was her, or at least her spirit, letting me know she was with us for Christmas.

If I did doubt this in any way, she looked straight into my eyes then turned to show me her back, before she took flight to the roof next door. There was something on her back that convinced me her spirit had truly come to let me know she was here and not to be sad. That something was a reminder of a time we shared before she passed.

Then, my daughter then told me, "It's been really weird, Mum. These cockatoos have been coming here for the last two weeks, sitting on the windowsill and watching us while we have breakfast, then disappearing until the next morning."

Call me crazy, which some of you probably already are, but I needed no more proof. Mum and I had been sharing Christmas breakfast together for over twenty years and the synchronicity of this was not lost on me. When I spoke with my daughter earlier today, Boxing Day, she also mentioned that the cockatoos had not come this morning.

*****

Now, let's begin. You will need to get a note pad and pen. Make up a chart like the one I have made, below. Then fill in the spaces you've created with any *signs* you know you have already. In the next column write in what they mean to you. Make sure you leave enough space to keep adding signs as they appear and to note what they mean. Once you have this list, it will be easier for you to begin trusting them, if you add a tick or something, so you can see the number of times, you see them, growing in front of you.

The list is your confirmation to yourself that it works. It is your proof. The example chart shows a couple that I have and have added how I *read* them and what their meaning is in my life.

There is no right or wrong answer. All signs are unique to each one of us in their meaning and timing. Some people can have the same sign as you but it might mean something different to them. This is because of their and your life experiences. We all have different experiences and these experiences provide our brain with meanings that are significant and unique to us alone.

EXAMPLES

Signs	Meaning
Black Cat	*Intuition* - Seeing a black cat or having one hang around you is usually a sign that you need to trust your intuition or your instincts about something going on in your life at that moment, e.g., making a decision, changing a job, etc.
Dogs	*Loyalty & Protection* – Animals come into our lives, sometimes it's planned and sometimes it's in unexpected ways. This has happened twice in our family and even although they have both now passed over, their loyalty and love remain in our lives to this day.

Signs	Meaning
Horses	*Strength* – reminders of strength, power of spirit, nobility, beauty and of delicious freedom. For me, horses are a reminder that just being me is enough. That by simply being is everything.
Dragonflies	*Transformation* - These beautiful creatures usually signal transformation. A change is coming. Welcome the change, feeling more joy in the way you view life in general. "...resonating the rainbow colours of frequency and light to create a powerful transformation of energy and consciousness...by opening your third eye and releasing self-doubt." (Transference Healing Animal Magic 2nd Ed. p.95)
Butterflies	*Change* – A reminder to see the beauty in your life. To know that growth and change are inevitable and that how you see yourself today is not necessarily how you will see yourself tomorrow.
Snakes	*Rebirth* – Represents a shedding of skin. Change and renewal.

Signs	Meaning
White Cockatoo	*Communication* - Is a symbol of communication. It is no accident that they can be trained in our vocal language. A white cockatoo flew straight at my windscreen, and then sat on a telegraph pole looking at me, as I went past. Then it swooped down and flew across the front of my car nearly causing me to have a heart attack, it came so close. This happened the afternoon Mum passed away and just after I had left her, and was driving back to her unit. Since then, I know it is a sign for me and usually comes when I'm undecided about something important to me. I believe it's Mum's way of saying take a breath or of just reminding me that she is still there if I need her.
Eagles	*Determined/Focused* - Be strong and determined. Keep your eye on the prize. The universe provides what you're focused on. Focus on what you want not what you don't want.
Rainbows	*A Symbol of Hope, New Life* - These are a symbol of hope, A washing away of the old to make room for the new. They breathe new life. This is what they mean to me. However, there are many meanings for rainbows and what they mean.

Signs	Meaning
Feathers	*Angels at Work* - These are little messages from our angels, to let us know that we're not alone. Sometimes, when I'm sad I will see a feather lying on the ground in front of me. The other day, for example, I was walking from my car to work. Something made me stop for a second, and a feather floated down right in front of me, so close I put my hand out and it landed in it. I know this was my angels telling me to stop worrying, as everything would be all right, and it is.
Number Plates	*Make Up Your Own Messages* - These are everywhere, but sometimes – if a car has cut in front of me, for example –I take in the number plate. As I'm reading it, I trust the first thing that comes to my mind. It's a message. Whether it guides me to something, or the numbers have a special meaning for me, or I make words out of the letters...say BLT000 sure there is the obvious or, Believe Love Trust Spirit. You can make a fun game of it on 'road trips' as well.

These are just a few examples and every time I see one, it lifts my spirits because I know I'm being watched over and there is help if I just ask for it. Of course, there are many other signs. Some that make me laugh at the unexpected timing of them. Some even happen after

I've forgotten that I asked for a sign. At other times, it doesn't matter what the signs are that are thrust in our face, they do this to try to wake us up to what we need to do, or something we need to look at.

We may not see the signs right in front of us. We may just be too busy being busy. When this happens... take a long slow breath; take three long slow breaths. Can you feel the subtle relaxation that weaves its way through your whole body, placing you into a state of peace and calm?

Once, before the children and I moved north, and before I had decided to sell my house, I had a frightening experience and it was definitely not one of peace and calm. I already knew it was not good for me to stay in the house for too long, but one night something strange happened.

I was sound asleep and at some time during the night, I thought I was dreaming as I felt something heavy on my chest and I couldn't move. I was also struggling to breathe. I was fighting to get whatever 'it' was off my chest. Then, just as I started to wake up I realised that even though I could see nothing, it was still there, like a truck crushing the breath out of me.

I came fully awake and was still struggling to move or to get breath into my lungs. I yelled. It was a squeak of a yell, but fuelled with anger. (Not fear, which surprised me when I thought about it later).

"Get off me, get off me, and get out of my house!"

I felt the weight lift off me. The next thing, it was gone and I couldn't *feel* it anywhere. I was so angry that something I couldn't even see had tried to suffocate me, although once it was gone, I felt nothing and life went on as normal. It did get me thinking about moving sooner rather than later.

A few days later I was telling a friend about it, and she told me it was a 'Chinese Sitting Ghost'.

I laughed, "You've got to be joking. That's the funniest thing I've heard."

"Look them up, if you don't believe me," she said.

"No, I don't need to do that. If that's true, then what does it mean?" I asked.

"They are steeped in myth and ancient Chinese traditions. They are a malevolent ghost that is supposed to sit on a person's chest, making it impossible for them to move or breath, and some of them even try to eat you. Scary huh?"

I let it go, but afterwards I did a quick bit of research online, and discovered that it is not just the Chinese, but in fact a huge number of different countries, that have their own *sitting ghost* stories, which are carried down through the centuries. If you happen to find this interesting, just put '*sitting ghost myth*' or '*reality*' into the search bar and have a look at what comes up.

*****

I'm pretty sure almost everyone has heard of the 'Parking Angels'. You ask them for a parking spot and then one appears just when you need it. Total trust and belief is needed here. But they can work in other ways too.

There maybe unexplained impulses to go right instead of left. To wait a longer time than you had intended to go shopping or whatever you intended. Then, later that day or the next day, you hear about an accident that kept the road you usually took jammed with traffic. You missed being caught because on impulse (or intuition) you went a different way at the last minute, or at a later time.

Perhaps you stayed home instead of going out with your friends. At the last minute, you didn't feel up to it. The next day a girlfriend rings and says "You were so lucky you didn't come last night, because..." The list goes on and I'm sure you have many intriguing examples of your own you could share.

If you don't, then it's time to start creating them. Listen! Listen out for when your intuition tries to guide you. Life flows more freely when you do. You can use your Sign Chart as proof by keeping a record of the number of times your intuition spoke to you and you listened. This proof can help give you the courage to begin acting on it.

*****

The following is a list of basis numbers. Numbers are everywhere and are a universal language.

NUMBERS – THE BASICS

000	Connection to Spirit: Know Spirit is around you and you can ask for their help.
111	Watch your thoughts. Make sure you're thinking about what you want in your life. Our thoughts are like magnets.
222	Have faith that all is at it should be, and everything is working out for you.
333	Ascended Masters are here to support you in major life decisions. Call on them often.
444	Angels, angels, angels are all around you, supporting you, and giving you encouragement to keep going.
555	A change is coming for you. Look forward to the changes in your life.
666	A time to feel grateful for all the miracles in your life. Treasure where you are right now.
777	Keep going. You are where you're meant to me and on the right path for your journey.
888	$$$$ Not only money but abundance in all areas of your life. Embrace abundance. You don't necessarily need to be financially wealthy to be wealthy.
999	Endings and new beginnings. Be filled with optimism, joy and wonder at all the blessings in your life.
1234 can be any consecutive numbers	Moving, house, job, or relationship. A big move/shift is on its way to you.

What I love about numbers is that they cannot lie. What you see is what you get. No matter how you read them, the answer is always their truth. I've put these numbers down as another way of looking for signs.

Now numbers can mean different things to different people, but the numbers themselves can tell you a truth about yourself in your life, if you're open to looking for *your truth* in them. I've included a couple of reference books about numerology, numbers, and meanings at the end for you. If this is your thing, have fun.

I've three more examples I'd like to share with you, that meant the world to me at the time they occurred. Being able to allow spirit to move through me is something that I don't take for granted, ever. Allowing words to be expressed through me to another is a gift I treasure and sometimes it surprises me more than I could ever know at the time.

Poppet: I had a friend in Avalon who worked in energy healing and we used to see each other every so often. Sometimes we shared our gifts with each other when one of us needed a little extra help with something.

She had a beautiful English accent even although she and her family had been living here for years. She was such a lovely person with a giving nature.

Our children grew up and left school, so we lost touch for a while as you sometimes do. It had been about a year, or maybe two, when I saw her again. I had gone back to Avalon one day and she was standing outside a deli/cafe talking to a friend of hers. Seeing Carlee, I hurried down the street towards her before she decided to go. I felt an urgency in my steps. As I approached her, she turned and saw me.

"Oh Karen it's so good to see you."

Before saying a word to her, I reached out and wrapped my arms around her, holding her close,

I said, "Don't worry Poppet, it will be alright. Everything is alright." Carlee held on to me for a few more seconds. When we took a step back and I looked at her she had tears in her eyes.

"What's wrong Carlee? Are you okay?"

"Oh you don't know do you?" she said.

Know what?" I asked.

"Karen, my dad passed away last week in England, and I didn't get a chance to go over to see him and say goodbye in person."

"I'm so sorry for you, I truly am Carlee," I said.

"It's okay," she replied. "I know he's okay now, thank you."

Puzzled, I asked, "For what?"

Apparently, I hadn't even realised what I'd said but then she told me..." My dad always used to call me Poppet and when I heard you say that, I knew it was my father letting me know it was okay, and he was okay."

It's experiences like these that fill my heart with gratitude and a profound humility. To be of help to someone when they are in need, even if unwittingly, is a blessing; a true gift to me.

****

Cookies & Hot Chocolate: This one is personal for me. It was going on two years since my dad had passed over, and it was my second Christmas without him. Time had kept moving on and the children had gone back to school and preschool after the Christmas holidays. When I arrived home, after dropping them off, I felt restless. Nothing I was supposed to do such as the washing, making beds or shopping was helping. I wanted to play hooky from my life.

So, I made myself presentable and went to Miranda Fair, to the movies. They always had a new one out after Christmas. I walked in feeling a bit guilty and after looking at what was on, I saw one that suited my time frame. I bought a ticket and made my way downstairs and into the cinema. I always liked to sit in the back row on the aisle seat, but there was an extremely large woman sitting there and she was eating. Nevertheless, I excused myself and went past her to sit a few seats away.

Once I had settled myself in and relaxed ready for the movie to start this smell hit me like a ton of bricks.

"Oh my God cookies, chocolate chip cookies, she must have bought them when they were just out of the oven" I said to myself. The smell was quite literally driving me crazy. I had to have some and even thought of asking her for one, but of course I couldn't. I stole a look at what was in her hand and saw she was eating chips not chocolate. What was going on here I wondered. The smell was so strong.

The movie began. It was *Michael* with John Travolta. I sat absorbed in the movie. When the people and a dog get to the house where Michael is supposed to be living they meet the owner, a woman played by Jean Stapleton. She is so funny and the perfect foil for the 'Archangel Michael' who is supposed to have come down to earth. This group were there to prove he was a hoax.

The point of this for me is while they were sitting down in the lounge room, waiting to meet him, the woman remarks on the smell of cookies that the owner is baking, but it is only bacon and eggs.

"Cookies," she says.

"Oh, that's Michael," is the answer. So, I'm sitting in the cinema thinking there is finally a rational explanation for this smell of chocolate cookies that I can still smell.

"I wonder how they can do that," I asked myself.

Once the movie finished and on my way out, I asked one of the ushers in passing, "Do you know how they do that with the cookie smell in the *Michael* movie?"

He said, "What smell?"

"The cookie smell in that cinema downstairs where the film's showing. I could smell cookies in the cinema" I told him.

He looked at me as if I was mad.

"There isn't any smell and if there is I'll send the cleaners down to check it out before the next session."

I was really confused. I got into my car to start driving home, when thoughts of my dad popped into my head.

"Hi Dad, your daughter's going mad." I said. Then a picture of a cup of hot chocolate was on the side of the road near a cafe and I finally got it.

"That was you, Dad!" It wasn't the woman, the movie or the cookies. It was my dad reminding me he was nearby and trying to remind me of our cafe times with hot chocolate and cookies.

It all finally made sense. I had been really missing my Dad that day and everything else was just my way, and his, of trying to connect. As I said, sometimes the *signs* can be rather cryptic or they can be so obvious you don't notice them until one of them is right in your face, like the cup of hot chocolate on the sign.

Some might say I'm just strange. However, our signs are important to us and our intuition is not as absolute as actual road signs for instance, but it is just as real. I know this with everything I am. Oh, and today 'Michael' is still one of my favourite movies to watch.

****

Guardian Angels: The final example happened quite a few years ago, after a woman came into where I worked. We began talking and she showed me some "Guardian Angels." I told her how beautiful I thought they were and she gave me one.

They were small crystal angels she made to wear on a chain or hang on a key ring. A week later I found out a dear friend had become very ill.

When this woman came back into work a few days later to pick up her order, I told her about my friend and asked if I could pay her to make an angel for me to give my friend. She must have been busy, because she pulled out a handful of them and told me to pick whichever one I liked. I did and gave it to my friend to help keep her feeling strong, safe and secure while she dealt with her illness.

Christmas was getting closer and one day before we broke up for holidays, this lovely woman came in again and gave me enough *angels* for my friend's family and for my family. She said she had also made a long crystal drop for my friend to hang on a window for the sunlight to shine on. It was magnificent with many different crystals used, all to enhance healing.

The following year, my son had to go away for work. He had a dangerous job, so I asked him take one of these *angels* with him for him, but mostly for me. He accepted my gift. I know he did this because he knew how much it meant to me, although I also sensed he was doing it for himself too. It was a small, tangible, physical object that I prayed would keep him safe and bring him home to me – to us – his family who loved him more than words can say.

I know the synchronicity of these three events *was divinely guided. They were truly looking after us. Timing is everything. Timing is always perfect!* How did that beautiful lady know I would be in need of more angels and, how did she know exactly how many?

So please, trust your *signs* and what they mean to you. Learn them, and learn their language off by heart. Hold it within your heart and you will learn and know so much more about yourself and your purpose in the process.

"Your work is going to fill a large part
of your life, and the only way
to be truly satisfied is to do what
you believe is great work.

And the only way to do great work
Is to love what you do.

If you haven't found it yet,
Keep looking. Don't settle.
As with all matters of the heart,
You'll know when you find it."

Steve Jobs 1955-2011

CHAPTER 16

Understanding

Everyone has their own identity and way of looking at things, and it is no different with your intuition. We all have our own experiences and our own history in the way we look at the world and how we then connect to the things around us. Testing out your intuition for yourself is a thing to have fun with.

I played games with mine, until I really believed that I was able to trust it in all the things in my life. It became a natural part of my thought process, and how I did things. Although, as I've said, except for a few exceptions, I didn't really begin in earnest until I was in my early forties and after Dad passed over.

It is wonderful to see how people, who are interested in trying to connect with their intuition, look and express what is happening when they see it working for themselves and this is the key. It is fine for someone else to tell you about something, but you need to experience it for yourself otherwise it remains an abstract that belongs to them. I cannot make it part of my understanding and knowledge base until I have the experience of it. I hope this is making sense to you?

In saying this, I would also like to point out that integrity is the most important ingredient in using your intuition to try to help someone. Remember the thoughts or visions you may get depend on how it works for you. Mostly, I find it will be an abstract that may not – probably will not – make sense to you.

However, the information you've been shown is not meant for you, so if you tell that someone exactly what you hear or see or feel, as it is shown to you, hopefully it will make sense to them. You may have had a 'vision' or 'felt' something or even heard a sound before it came into your reality. The thing is we all have these kinds of experiences throughout our lives. Whether you choose to believe it or pass it off as a coincidence is your choice.

Once, when I was a little girl, living in the Western suburbs of Sydney, I was watching the news on TV (because that is what my dad was watching at the time). The story was about the bad weather and it showed the Manly Ferry, telling how it was late because of the fog that had settled over Sydney Harbour. The picture on the screen showed passengers disembarking.

I said to my dad "Wouldn't it be wonderful to be able to travel to work by ferry?" As a girl growing up in the Western suburbs, this was not something that I could EVER imagine being able to do. I would be a train person for my working life. At least that is what I knew at the time.

I would never have believed I would be doing this. But, what if just the fact of uttering those words, and the feeling I put into them as well as the images of me tasting the salt spray as it splashed up over the bow of the ferry and onto my face, (all happening for me in the seconds while voicing those words), what if? What if this was enough to begin creating the life for me that it did, somewhere many years down the track. It eventually became part of my life for a year or two, and I never got tired of making this trip from Manly to the City. After years of train travel, riding the Manly Ferry was a magical way for me to go to and from work. Did I create it, or was it just a coincidence?

In my world, there are no coincidences and the words you use and the feelings you put into them are very powerful and have energy of their own. In your world, you may not be or become psychic! You can however trust, or learn to trust, the signs that you see; the signals your intuition sends you.

"Why would I want to do this?" you ask. Well to answer that, if you're reading this book I think it is pretty obvious. You are curious and curiosity is a wonderful thing. Curiosity stretches our mind and expands our thinking process. I keep saying everyone has a gift and it is true. You know it is true, because if you know what yours is, you know it and if you don't, you know it is still something you're looking for.

If you allow yourself to begin trusting the innate wisdom you hold inside, which speaks to you through the voice of intuition, it will guide you through signs and signals that hold recognition and meaning for you to act on. All you need to do is be aware, so that when things, or signs, present themselves to you, you actually notice them and pull them into your conscious mind.

Once spirit sees that you're taking notice of them, even if you may not quite understand what they mean to you at that time, spirit will keep putting more and more signs into your path, until you start to see a pattern forming. Your pattern will be different from mine, because your life and the way you live it is different from mine. But eventually you will learn to understand their meaning.

Before my father passed, he told me that he would always be around to watch over my children and I took so much comfort in this. On a night, about a year after Dad died, when my daughter was around two-and-a-half, I was tucking her into bed. Part of our usual routine was to sing her favourite song, Twinkle, Twinkle Little Star, together. This particular night, however, she was distracted and kept looking over my shoulder.

"What's the matter, Sweetheart?" I asked.

She pointed to a corner in her room and said, "Granda."

"Grandad," I said.

She nodded.

"How do you know its Grandad, honey?"

"Orange sparkles, Mummy."

I looked, but didn't see anything, although I know young children can see things that we cannot.

She said, "See him Mummy, orange sparkles?"

"Does Grandad come to see you every night?" I asked her.

She nodded her head and then turned over and I tucked her in and kissed her goodnight. As I turned to leave her room, I looked into the corner where she had pointed and said, "Thanks Dad. I love you." Then, I left the room knowing Dad was looking after my children just as he told me he would. I never saw the sparkles, but that didn't matter, because spirit presents itself to us in a language we can understand, whatever our age or experience.

For me, our contact came through writing and the smell of ink. Let me explain. When I was very young, my father owned a printing shop. He also published a newspaper he called 'The Courier'. As a family, we delivered it once a week to the local neighbourhood, and then further afield as the readership began to expand. As I grew older, the business became a halfway stop between high school and home. Every afternoon I got off the bus and stayed at the shop with Dad, until he was ready to go home.

I loved being here and he put me to work, of course, dusting invitations and the like, while the smell of the inks he used filled the shop and my nostrils. I loved watching him set the type in the machines, ready to start printing the paper. It was so exciting to watch and to be a part of this. The point is, if I close my eyes, I can still smell that ink and see my father working there. So you see writing and ink are our link.

When you start to listen to your intuition and the signs begin appearing in your life, don't just notice them, and think "Oh isn't that weird" or "What a coincidence I was just thinking of that person."

Trust that you're noticing it for a reason and the reason doesn't need to mean something huge. It could be that you were thinking you should call that person to arrange to catch up, and your intuition was just confirming it was a good thought, or reinforcing the thought so you would remember to make the catch up happen.

Intuition works with you, not against you. When you allow it to be in your life, it can make your life a whole lot simpler. It's like your phone that you can't leave home without. Intuition is a diary that reminds your mind not your eyes and ears. As I keep saying, I AM just like you, but I trust my internal GPS as much as most people trust the external GPS in their car.

*****

Have you ever felt that some days you may as well be hitting your head against a brick wall? Well these are the times, or the signs, that tell you you're going the wrong way, or further away from where you might want to be. They are not as obvious as – say – going the wrong way on a freeway, where they actually have signs telling you "WRONG WAY GO BACK" but I'm sure you get my drift. These are also the times in our lives when anxiety starts to creep in, or you may start feeling depressed because something you wanted to work out didn't.

There are many reasons why we can be thrown off course. In my experience, even if you think you can't take some time out, or you don't have time, or whatever the excuse you tell yourself is, these are the moments where meditation can come in handy. As I talked about in Chapter 10, meditation is a wonderful way to calm your mind and body so you can connect with your inner self. If you work in an office, close the door for five minutes to do some deep breathing. This in itself can really help you to slow a racing heart rate, if done with awareness. Most of all, deep breathing, and meditation can have a similar outcome in that they get you to sit still and be in that moment.

This helped in moving my focus, to the things I found important in my life and learning more about the things that excited me, was how I wanted to devote my time and my energy. I was still in a caring role and looking after others, but now, the more I learnt about myself, the more I felt I might be able to help other people empower themselves in their own lives.

I remember a reading I did for a client where the outcome was a very positive one for the client and for myself.

As she was leaving, she turned to me and asked "When do I need to come back to see you?"

Her question threw me for a moment then I told her "If I have done my job properly, you won't need or want to come back to see me." As she walked off, I could tell that she didn't quite know what to make of it.

She had been to other psychics who had encouraged her to come back. That is not my role. My role is to empower people, so they can live better and more fulfilled lives using the tools they have at their disposal. I know what it is to live a disempowered life, and to feel as if all of your choices have been taken away from you. Now, I also know that to be able to feel empowered and to take charge of your own life is the most important gift you can give yourself. I know you can and will find what works for you.

If you're here, now, living this life, I guarantee you already are perfect and everything you need is already within you. However, most of us walk through life thinking we're not perfect, but how could we be anything else, anything less? When do we stop being perfect? How can we learn to be less than that?

Look at a newborn child. Feel the feeling you have when you are a witness to their perfection. When does that child stop being perfect? Is there a time limit? In the eyes of a parent, their child is perfect forever. So when or how does that child come to think of itself as anything less than perfect?

I believe we stop looking at ourselves that way the minute another's words make us feel pain or hurt. It might be the result of thoughtless words, thrown our way by another child, or an adult, or and adult/child. The adult/child has been hurt in a similar way before, but had no reference with which to address the pain it caused and they carry it around with them – sometimes, for their whole life. This tragedy can be caused simply by a lack of understanding. I see that we are all perfectly unique, yet also so similar in so many ways, as human beings. Although this should be embraced, sadly it is not always so.

If there is no conversation, no explanation, or no truth, this pain or hurt can plant a seed of doubt that can grow to cloud and distort your understanding of yourself. This kind of behaviour needs a conversation based on truth and ownership.

Any conversation that strives for truth and ownership can resonate from a base of compassion. This in turn can help the participants to garner understanding, compassion, and trust. It leaves no room for feelings of doubt or guilt on either side. I feel this is the way towards keeping and embracing our perfection. By widening the perspective, we allow a greater understanding of the other. By allowing a greater understanding, in honest and truthful conversations, we can help each other to recognise, embrace, and keep nurturing one another.

I've always seen the heart of a person. Their outside is inconsequential. This has been the cause for a lot of heartache for me, on the physical level, and of enormous joy. It is the feeling I get when I meet someone new, or when I try to surround myself with friends who are being true to themselves, as I also strive to do.

I've never had time for chatty conversations, where people talk and talk but never really say anything. If you haven't already guessed, I'm not good at parties.

Life is so short. I prefer to converse with people who are interesting and interested in people and in living their best and most authentic life. For some this may include a party or two. Your life is about what it right for you. I speak only for myself. For me, words are meaningless if there is no truth or heart to propel them.

"Tears cast shadows upon the road ahead,
clouding my judgment and moving me
into a realm, where I'd rather not go.
I watch them fall from a place
of separation.

I move into an awareness,
of my soul and its limitless possibilities.
I understand the tears
and their need to fall.

Thereby, expressing one small particle
of the soul essence that is I.

Looking, then, with incredible wonder
at the responses, I take myself through
to further my journey.
Step by step
I find the puzzle that was
unfolding before me,
as I breathe in its magnificence!"

Karen N Sawyer 2000

332

CHAPTER 17

Chaos to Calm

How do we change the negatives in our lives to positives? I've come to understand that I cannot continue to look at my life in this way. Words and actions each have a field of energy attached to them and, depending on the connotations we place on our words and actions, that energy will be either negative or positive.

The further into this road trip I get, the more I realise that life is about our perception of things; the 'view' from which we look at them and the kind of energy we place on them. Let's face it, unless we're in a really happy place at a particular time, most people tend to allow the negative things to swallow them up and they wallow in that space until they can stand it no longer. This is while the happy, wondrous things tend to be taken for granted and looked at with a "I can't believe I got so lucky" kind of view. Does any of this resonate with you? Can you think of a time in your life when this kind of thinking was how you looked at those circumstances?

I remember a long time ago, when I was in my twenties, a girlfriend of mine went travelling to Europe for a year. After she returned, she told me how wonderful her trip had been. One of the places she went was Paris. I admit I was a little envious, for I too wanted to go there. While she was telling me about her trip, the part that stuck in my mind was how she was described her 'view' of Paris.

The words she used were "unless I could get down in the gutter, I don't feel I would have seen the 'real' Paris." Now whether these were her actual choice of words or not it was a long time ago so I can't be sure. However this is what I heard, at least my 'view' of what I heard'.

I did get to Paris a few years later and 'gutter' was the last word ever to cross my mind. Majestic, awe-inspiring were my words, and I walked through the many streets of Paris finding all of her hidden delights. What I'm getting at is we both went to Paris, we both walked through the streets of Paris, but we described our journey in different ways. I'm quite sure we both left Paris filled with similar feelings about our times there. Which description was wrong? Neither! How we each experienced the things we saw and what happened to us, as well as how we choose to describe them, were exactly our choice.

Right, wrong, positive or negative; the perception of what another person says is possibly something we may need to address, if our thinking keeps placing it within the binary of positive verses negative.

In this example, I would be placing my friend's view into my negative framework, while placing my view into my positive framework. This kind of thinking only separates. However, if I look at this example through the vision of my internal spiritual light, there is no separation. This is love. This is total understanding and acceptance and this is changing negative thinking into positive.

The further down this road I go, the closer I come to understand that everything I did, witnessed or felt was a choice I made, through the view of where I was in that moment. Things happen to all of us as we go through our lives. However, it is how we choose to look at what is happening and how we deal with it that counts.

Most obviously, hindsight is our best teacher. Distance and time always give us perspective, as well as influencing how we view those things that come back into our memories. If we've kept learning throughout our lives, we can eventually come to view the things that happened 'to' us with compassion and understanding. We are able to see why we responded as we did, or why we acted out as we did.

Growth, true growth comes when we're able to look back with an understanding of the other person or persons' view or to see the reasons why they acted as they did. Sometimes, this can be very hard, even from a distance, because we all feel justified about our feelings. However, true growth as a human being is being able to place yourself in the other person's shoes and to see their world through their eyes. Only then, can we understand and feel compassion for those who we felt 'wronged' us – or for that matter – whom we may have wronged.

Have you ever noticed how sometimes it can be easier to forgive someone else than it might be to forgive yourself? This doesn't need to apply to the big things in life, either. Sometimes, it can be as small as eating a chocolate bar when you told yourself you wouldn't. Oh, the guilt that follows can hang around you for days, while you beat yourself up emotionally. Get over it! I say eat the chocolate bar, enjoy it at the time, and then let it go. Otherwise, the guilt will eat through you far longer than the silly chocolate bar took to eat.

As I've said, and will keep saying, justification is a word that is thrown around to place blame on others or to exonerate ourselves from blame. We are all trying to do the best we can with the knowledge we have at any given time.

As humans, we're not infallible, but when we're able to come from that place of spiritual awareness that resides deep within all of us, and to take action from within this space, only then can we recognise that the same light of God shines in us all. We are the children; the brothers and sisters who can shine this light out all over the world. There is no darkness that can hide when light is present. Darkness exists so that light can be seen and there can be no light without darkness to reveal its presence. They are an example of binaries moving within a supportive structure so that both can exist.

When we place a person, or action, into the 'other', this language allows us to separate that, which we view or think of as different, from ourselves. If we can learn to view this 'other' as a part of the whole (in whatever example you choose), albeit a part we may not want to look at. If we can change our thinking of this part we view as negative, and, if we can bear witness to the positive in someone or something else, then acceptance, growth and love become our main focus and intention.

*****

I used to read a book to my children, as they were growing up. It was written by Neale Donald Walsh and it spoke of the light of God, and how we're all a part of that light. Neale describes this as "a very profound truth: there is no absolute good or bad – that underneath all that happens in the world, all that we call 'good' and all that we call 'bad', is 'love'." In this parable, one of the little souls in heaven wants to experience what it feels like to be the light he/she already knows they are. This little soul goes to God and says;

"Well, you're God. Think of something!"

God smiled. "I already have... since you cannot see yourself as the Light when you are in the Light, we'll surround you with darkness."... God explained that, in order to experience anything at all, the exact opposite of it will appear. "It is a great gift... because without it, you could not know what anything is like... And so, when you are surrounded with darkness, don't shake your fist and raise your voice and curse the darkness. Rather be a Light unto the darkness, and don't be mad about it. Then you will know Who You Really Are...," N.D. Walsh (1998) pp. 5–9.

This children's parable goes on to show how the little soul experiences being and feeling. I haven't thought of that book, since my children were small, but now I've begun reading it to my granddaughter.

I'm sure we all have examples of times in our lives, which we can look back on from here. As an exercise, I ask that you revisit one of those experiences of yours. If it is a fair way back, you should be able to take the emotion out of your viewpoint. Try to view it from the perspective of an onlooker, who does not know you and all the baggage you carried with you at that time.

Now take a pen and a piece of paper and write down what you're looking at as a conversation, using logic. Write down what you hear, write down what you see. Then, write about the feelings the conversation gives you as a whole.

However, before you do any of this, place someone else in your role. You have to be your own devil's advocate. When you've finished, put it down. Then go for a walk, a swim, have a cup of tea, a chat with a friend, or watch a movie. Just don't read what you've written down, until you've also placed some distance between you and what is written on the paper. Even better would be to wait until the next day, after life's business has removed it from your thoughts.

Then, after the morning rush is over, sit down where you will not be disturbed and read it back and let it settle. Then do the exercise over again, only this time using what you wrote down on that piece of paper. Write any thoughts, or feelings etc. that arise from this.

The point of this exercise is to be able to get to a place where you can see yourself and the other person from the same viewpoint. In other words no negative no positive. Let me know how you go. But, before you do, I want you to go through this whole process again, using something that is happening in your life at this moment. That's right and it will be the first thing that pops into your head, now.

PS: I will be doing this too, and we will be allowing our intuition to guide us along the way.

*****

I once met a young boy at a party. It was a children's party. All the children were off running all over the yard. I went inside to get some water, and I saw this little boy sitting in the kitchen.

"What's the matter?" I asked. "Don't you want to go and play with all the other kids?"

"I'm playing. I'm playing hide and seek with him," he said pointing to a space near the door where I had come in.

"But I can't see anyone honey."

"Yeah see, there he is."

It was then that I understood. How many children have invisible friends and how many times do we tell them they don't? It didn't matter that I couldn't see what he saw, what he heard, or what he felt. What mattered was that he trusted me enough to let me into the world he lived in, if only for a moment. I was aware enough to know we all experience this other side in different ways.

Interrupting my thoughts as though he had heard them, he said, "It's just a game we play. Don't tell Mum. She doesn't understand." He laughed as he ran off into another room.

Children come into our world as complete *miracles*. Our role, our only role is not to screw them up while they are under our care. They are whole and they are perfection. All we're asked to do is to help them grow; softly guiding them, and allowing them enough space, love and support to choose their own path, their own destiny. Listen to them, to the voice we already recognise the minute they begin to speak.

My five-year-old granddaughter was with me today, so I asked her what she thought we all need to be happy. This is what she said.

"We all need love and cuddles, because they make us feel happy and safe.
We also need trees to make the air we breathe.
We all need water to hydrate and food to eat, and we need a home to live in."

Simplistic? Yes, but the simple answers are usually the right ones. We must trust that the children, who are to be the new caretakers of this earth, know where they are going and what they need to do to get there.

Changing our perspective starts with our children and starts with us, each one of us today, in this moment. Look for the good in everything that crosses your path today. Take in the feeling you have or get inside. Stop and find a positive you can take away from it.

Look to our children, and learn from them in the way they embrace and expand in the moments throughout their day. We need to be open to learning, for perceptions and perspectives to change.

*****

I wasn't going to include this, but, I was at my dentist this morning and our old family home, where Matt and I lived with our children, was just around the corner. It was only a ten-minute drive from the courthouse we attended a long time ago. It is such a funny story; I kind of wanted to revisit it for you. It's the court case I referred to earlier in Chapter 11.

We were all at the courthouse. By we, I mean my solicitor; my sister, as a witness, and our friend, Jane. Then there was Matt and his solicitor, of course, and the rest of the gallery in the courthouse. This courthouse was a very new building and nothing like the old, dark, gloomy one they used to have in the city.

The room we were in was very bright with light panelled walls and a huge skylight running the length of the ceiling, from the entry door to the magistrate's bench. It was also a beautiful sunny day with not a cloud in sight. It certainly was not reflective of the reason we were all there that day, which was Matt. After all those years, he had made a mistake, and now I had a witness to his extreme behaviour. We were all asked to stand. The magistrate entered and took her place and we all sat down before the formal proceedings began.

I was to give my evidence first, and even though I had spent half my working life amongst the legal profession, I could still feel my knees shaking as I walked up and into the witness box. In this courthouse, you were raised higher than anyone else was in the room, except for the magistrate, of course.

As I answered the questions put to me by both sides, I tried not to look at Matt and focused my gaze on the solicitors and the beams of sunlight shining into the room, which created an angelic hue. I had not asked my angels for help today.

I was too distracted and on edge to think of them, but looking at the sunlight pouring in, I could feel their presence supporting me. By the time we finished my testimony and that of my sister, it was lunchtime. Court was dismissed for an hour, and we were all due back at 02:00pm, for Matt to take his turn in the witness box.

Once outside there was a rush to all the eateries to get tables. I prayed that we would be at a different one from Matt and his solicitor, and we were, so I could relax while we ate. We discussed how my solicitor thought it was going. On the way back into court, I tried to relax and just to soak in the warmth of the beautiful day we'd been blessed with.

It took a while for everyone to settle back in as we waited for the magistrate to return. The gallery was full of other people hoping their matters would also get dealt with that day. The magistrate entered, took her seat, and called the courtroom to order. Then, Matt was asked to take the stand to give his evidence. Just as he was about to speak, a loud rumble seemed to shake the courthouse. The skies opened up and torrential rain pelted down on the roof.

A clap of thunder made most of us jump out of our seats, then a flash of lightening seemed to come straight through the sunroof giving the room an eerie brightness, but only for a second. The roar of the thunder and lightning combined made it impossible to hear anything else. Looking around the room, I saw most people were looking shocked and nervous as I was. It was very frightening being, what seemed to be, directly under the noise of the weather outside.

The magistrate asked Matt's solicitor to begin again, and he did. As each question was asked Matt answered with his usual flair for the dramatic, expunging any blame on his part. On and on he went, virtually spitting his answers out. All I could think of was I'm glad there was no one near him. The new scene, created by the weather, made him look like a preacher giving a sermon on hell and damnation to his flock. The stage had been created by the extremely sudden change in the weather.

The courtroom, and Matt's evidence giving were taking on the macabre feeling of a black comedy. However, it wasn't until that last couple of questions that things really erupted in the room.

Matt seemed to be revelling in the fact that he now had a captive audience, and that we were all being forced to listen the vitriol he was spouting. For the most part, I was embarrassed for him and the way he looked. I had heard everything he was saying so many times I'd become used to it in an odd way, but today there was a new element to his sermon. His solicitor finished questioning him and my solicitor stood up. All the while, the storm outside threatened to break the skylight and the noise had us sitting on the edge of our seats in case the walls caved in and we had to make a run for it.

At this point Matt's eyes were nearly bulging out of his head.

My solicitor said, "Now, Mr Tanner, you have sat here for the past twenty minutes telling us all these terrible things my client has done to you, is this right?"

"Yes, that's right Your Honour," he said with a smirk on his face, looking straight at the magistrate.

"Oh my God" I thought. He thinks he can charm her like everyone else.

"Excuse me Mr Tanner! Could you please address your answers to me. Now, why do you think that my client would want to do these things to you?" I could see Matt trying to think of how to answer.

"Well, to tell you the truth, I think she must be menopausal or something."

I broke out laughing so hard at this answer, I nearly chocked. I held up some papers in front of my face to try to hide behind. But, by then I noticed it was not only me laughing but also my sister and Jane. Matt's words and demeanour had brought down the entire courtroom. The magistrate who was not exactly laughing, though, in fact she was looking rather angry. Anyway, the laughter took a while to settle down, and the magistrate put her gavel down to stop everyone so my solicitor could continue.

A few giggles could still be heard throughout the rest of Matt's testimony. Just like that, all of the fear and anxiety I had vanished, as I became witness to the absurdity of it all.

Oh! I must tell you one more thing. The minute Matt got off the stand, I kid you not, the storm went away, as quickly as it had arrived and the sunlight shone down through the skylights again. When we left to go home, there was no evidence of the storm outside. This had happened in a normal suburban area of Sydney, where tropical weather was unheard of. So you tell me, do you think this could have been coincidence or a sign?

"Speak not in a tongue, which harbours
a grudge or envy.
You must be still and lovingly let others
dance their own dance.

We can but watch, until the movements
blend together.
A creation apart from all else
in this realm of endless possibilities.

Take up the stand to give and receive love,
Only love!
It is the essence sought for by all,
Even you...

Taking up the gauntlet is by no means
an easy task.
To stand fast in your own truth,
when those around pull and push,
shaking your vibrations to the core.

Know your strength and be at peace
in the reality that is you.
For you are an Angel,
highest of the high, and mere mortals
cannot distract you from your journey."

Karen N Sawyer 2000

CHAPTER 18

Your Path

In the time of Covid-19, we acknowledge the huge importance of our first responders. They are the people you think of when you're in need and we've needed them more than ever during the past couple of years. The fires, flooding, and now Covid-19 have all made us truly understand the depth of their commitment to their fellow beings. How can we not feel grateful and respectful of the position they place themselves in for their communities each and every day.

So what about you, and what about me?

How can we contribute to help our families, our friends, and the communities we live in? Now more than ever, we need to find the courage to discover what is special about each of us and to find out how we can use this knowledge to help our fellow human beings and ourselves. Don't settle for a mediocre life, when you have the potential residing within you to create a powerful and magnificent life. Whatever your gift is now is your time to shine! When you give yourself permission to shine, this will give others permission to do the same. In a world that is currently so damaged, if all we can do is shine our light out into the darkness, don't you think we should?

*****

There are many avenues available to you. Once you discover what interests you, ask for things to come into your life. It helps to be as specific as possible. Throw it out there into the universe. After all, no one else has to know what you've decided, and it's probably better that they don't.

You don't want anyone telling you that you can't. This is the fragile birthing of your ideas. It might seem easy for me to sit here and say this, however I promise you will know when you feel it.

Once you do this, embrace it, and decide that no other life will do. You will understand and the words you come up with for yourself will encompass the life. It can be the most exciting life you could dream of or wish for, and it is up to you to make it happen. Write it down on a piece of paper, fold it up, and put it somewhere safe – somewhere special. Some people like to bury it in their garden with the intent that their wishes will grow.

I actually like creating vision boards, although I used to write lists and found they always worked, as well. What is important is that it is your true heart connection, telling you, 'This is it! This is what I long to do.' Once you've made this your goal, the universe starts sending things, ideas, and people your way to help you. Why? Because every being on this planet needs you and what you have to share!

I remember, a while ago now, as my children were getting older, the unit we were living in became too small. My daughter and I had to share a room for a number of years and she was turning thirteen the following year. All she wanted was a room of her own. I had promised her she would have a room of her own by the time she turned thirteen.

I had no idea how I was going to afford the rent for a three-bedroom house or apartment. However, I knew her request was not unreasonable and somehow it was going to happen for her. She also wanted her own computer, but I told her that would have to wait.

I wrote a list of everything I *have* in our new home. The present tense was me accepting that it was already mine and that I knew all I had to do was to get out of my way and allow the universe to bring it to me. I cut out pictures of things such as the colour, floorboards with large rugs, a comfy lounge, large rooms, windows with a nice view, an outdoor balcony, my favourite trees, and plants, and even a colourful bowl of fruit on a kitchen bench. I put them all with the list into a folder named 'Our New Home' and forgot about it.

Christmas came and went and the children spent a few weeks down south on a holiday with their dad. A week before they were due to come home, I was sitting on the balcony drinking tea and reading the Saturday paper. I was flicking through the rentals when an advertisement caught my attention. Three-bed, upper duplex, Narrabeen, and although the price was more than what I was paying at the time, it was definitely way under what I thought I might have to pay. I had literally fifteen minutes to get there and have a look before the inspection time closed. I grabbed my bag, keys and ran down the stairs, jumped into my car and off I went. I made it with seven minutes to spare.

I walked in. There was no one else in the house. I looked around. It had everything I had put on my list, plus water views of the lake. My favourite ghost gum tree was in the front yard and a hot pink bougainvillea climbed over the balcony rail upstairs. The bathroom had pale green tiles, all except for two. One was a white magnolia and the other had a picture of a pink poodle, exactly like the poodle my Mum had just given my daughter for Christmas.

There were signs everywhere telling me this was our new home. All I needed to find was the third bedroom, which I did, down the stairs.

It was a huge room with outside access through the garage and perfect for an eighteen year old. If this wasn't enough, I was actually locked in by the agent. I made my way out and found her at the bottom of the driveway getting ready to leave. I asked her for an application form, took it home, filled out, and dropped in into their office before closing that day. Two days later, on the Monday afternoon, the agent called to tell me I had the duplex.

There is a feeling I get when I am on a purpose. Things flow smoothly and anything I need to do, to *make it happen*, feels effortless. I phoned the kids and told them that we were moving. Two weeks later, we were settled into our new home, exactly two weeks before my daughter turned thirteen. Oh, and on our first night in our new home, one of our new neighbours walked up the driveway carrying an Apple computer.

They said, "I was going to throw this out, but if you would like it, take it it's yours." You can guess what my daughter said.

I know when it is right or meant for me, and you will too. Everything flows smoothly and swiftly. As I said above, make some time to sit down and write out all the things you would like to do. Then read it back to yourself and see which stands out the most to you and the feelings you have around it. Please don't allow your ego or your logical thought process to get in the way.

Is there something that you used to do as a child that you don't get enough time to do now? Is there something you've always wanted to do, but never thought you could? Sometimes our 'gift' might be something that feels like a secret, or something, where you think others might say 'You can't do that', or you think they might laugh at you.

This idea that you've had might seem so fragile or so unattainable that you might not even voice it out loud to yourself, in case it disappears. That is when you know!

The creation of an idea is an extremely fragile time, at least to you. It will feel that way until you've fully-formed your idea of what you truly want to do with your life, so that it feels like a solid object and has grown some roots. Sometimes the most important thing we can do, when we finally know what it is that we want to do, is say nothing to others. Your spirit guides on the other hand will be standing around you smiling and excited that you've listened to your intuition, the innate wisdom of your soul.

If you're not sure how to get started, look for someone who is in the same, or a similar field, as the one you want to get into. There a plenty of people out there who want to help others. Once you know what you want to do, make another vision board. Put all the things on it that you will need to do, to get, and everything that will help keep your focus on it.

Remember an idea is like a seed. It needs nurturing before it can begin growing, but if someone stomps on it before that, there will be no growth. You may even throw the seed away. So plant the seed and allow the roots to make a home deep in the earth.

Thus, as it begins to grow what lies underneath is strong enough to withstand whatever weather comes its way. You and the life you envision for yourself is this seed. You must have faith in yourself, know yourself, and trust in yourself enough not to let what anyone says shake your resolve and your faith.

If this year has taught me anything it is that life is precious. Don't waste another minute of yours doing something you don't love, just to pay the bills. You could be doing something you do love. I should probably clarify this. I'm not telling you to leave a stable job, *especially when people are losing their jobs and businesses are currently going under.* What I am saying is this. Be grateful for every moment in your life, but right now – especially right now – there is every reason to begin taking steps towards creating the life you already know you love, until it manifests itself. No one else can do this for you. *YOU* need to take the necessary steps towards making it manifest in your life.

So it could be a job you want, a business you want to start; it might be that you need to study to get a degree; or you want a life partner, who hasn't shown up yet. Whatever your best life looks like to you, and whatever you need to do to make it happen, start today. Take control of your life. It's your gift and it is why you came here, so why not use it. Whether you believe it, yet, or not, you need to do it for yourself and your self-worth.

*****

I'm including a couple of examples of what we've been talking about in this chapter.

A girl came to see me. She was tired of meeting men who didn't want a relationship.

"Write down all the qualities you would like in a partner and place it somewhere in your house, and then forget about it," I said. She was a little unsure but I said, "That's it. You don't need to do anything else."

It is rare to get feedback about the readings I do, but every now and then, I have. This girl came back a few months later, to tell that she had needed a plumber. When he turned up he knocked on the window in the living room. He'd seen her as he was walking down the side path. She told me that after he finished the job, he asked her out. He turned out to be everything she had written down on her list. The best part was that she told me she had put the paper in a small antique vase and placed it on the windowsill. The same one they'd met over. Now that's what I call exact.

Another time, I had a young woman come to me for a reading. She was in a rowing team at a surf club and had been offered a position at a neighbouring club. She was very happy where she was, and wanted to know whether she should move. I asked her why she was uncertain about what to do, if she was happy where she was.

She said, "I'm not. I just have a feeling that I should move to this new club."

What I could see was that she knew she needed to move, but because she didn't actually have a reason, she felt unsure. As we went on, it became obvious that she was ready to start a new and more fulfilling personal relationship. As soon as this became evident, I also knew that the way to meeting this person was by going to the new club. If she stayed where she was, they would miss out on each other.

I told her, "There is a man there for you, and you're destined to meet him. That is why you're feeling as you do. He has long, blond hair and you will meet him within two weeks of starting there."

She felt better about her decision to move clubs, and left feeling better than when she came in. If she had just trusted what her intuition was telling her there wouldn't have been a need to come to see me. She would not have needed any proof that the move was the right thing to do. She would have accepted that moving was right for her, even although she didn't 'know' why at the time.

She would have accepted that along the way she would start a new relationship, after they met each other at the new club. She had already 'told' the universe what she wanted and her intuition had been trying to tell her '*if you want this new relationship you need to move because there is someone there who wants the same things as you do*'. Intuition is not an exact science, but when the energies align, powerful things can and do happen.

About seven months later, I was at my friends shop. She said, "I have a letter for you from a woman you did a reading for. She dropped it off the other day and asked me to pass it on to you."

"Thanks," I said, although I was a bit surprised and puzzled about whom it could be from. I opened the letter and read...

"Dear Karen,

I wanted to let you know that I did find someone after I started at the new surf club. He is a beautiful man. He is also on the rowing team, but on another boat and we've been going out for about six months and are doing great.

He doesn't have long, blond hair though. It's brown, but when we met, it was raining and he had a hooded yellow raincoat on. I thought that was really funny and wanted you to know you were right. Thank You"

*****

Those earlier examples were easy ones. But, what about the ones that are not that easy. What about the relationships we've had, on the way to finding our life partners? Our intimate relationships teach us a lot about who we are, and who we want to be, and this goes for both partners. It is my belief that the basis of any good relationship is honesty. I'm not saying that you need to give someone you've just met a *'warts and all'* version of who you are straight up front.

Maybe start with learning more about yourself. Make a list of say, five things you like about yourself. If there are more, keep on writing them down. Then, write a list of what you don't like about yourself. Now you know what you do and don't like about yourself. Ask yourself why for each of these attributes, starting with the 'like list'.

Then, go on to the 'don't likes'. Look at the don't likes list and ask yourself why you don't like these things. Really think about the *why* because being able to be honest with yourself, is important and necessary

The 'don't likes' are probably what are holding you back from being the person you are and the person you like. Tell the pain, you've been carrying' to carry its own bags and you will begin to feel joy and laughter again. You can be you, the one you love to be. Once the pain is gone, and the walls you've been hiding behind start coming down, you will be ready, when the right person comes along.

It is not just about the things we say to each other. A lot about relationships can be learnt about in the things we don't say. The things we may be too afraid to say, especially if you're already emotionally invested in that relationship. You really need to learn to trust your instincts – your intuition – because it will be speaking to you all along the way.

*" If we cannot have
faith and trust in ourselves,
how can we expect others to ?"*

CHAPTER 19

How to Trust

If you're anything like me, you will want proof that you really are doing what you think you are. Sometimes I find the proof I need through logic, and sometimes through the illogical or the unexplainable. As I mentioned earlier, in the first reading I ever had, I gave nothing of myself away, because I wanted proof. The proof I received came by way of the unexplainable. How could Freya know what she so obviously did?

Later, of course, I realised how hard it was and how much energy I made that poor girl use, just so I could get 'proof' that what she was doing for me was *real*. I got that because everything she told me was *true* and for me – at that time – it was totally illogical how she could know this. Yet I believed, because I had received the *proof* I needed.

This is the most important piece of the intuitive puzzle. You must be left in no doubt whatsoever that what happened did happen, and that what was said was absolutely true for you. In the beginning, it's hard enough to get your head around what is real and what is just your imagination. However, everything that is real begins in someone's imagination, and your imagination and intuition each work within the person that is you. Each work separately and, they also work together as a team.

Before you can trust anyone, anything, or the signs around you, you must learn to trust yourself. Maybe you already do. If that is so, you're already ahead of many people.

Trusting yourself starts with learning who you are. Who are you when the world falls away and it's just you and your thoughts. The questions I asked you, in the previous chapter, are also because of this. Your soul knows what its truth is, and that truth is yours to know and to access whenever you want. It is always your choice.

Our thoughts tell us a lot about who we are. Are you happy to spend time with yourself, or do you need others around to feel like you? The people you spend your time with are a reflection of who you are. Are you happy with who you see in the mirror each morning? Are there some big or small changes you may like to make? I'm not talking about physical changes. I'm talking about something much deeper than the skin. Only you have the answers to these questions.

As Louise Hay (1984) (founder of Hay House Publishing) always said, "People do your mirror work!" I have and it's taken me twenty years to be able to look in my mirror and smile and feel happy about *whom* I see in there and that has nothing to do with what I look like.

When you look into your eyes, you see your soul. If you're smiling, chances are your life is happy and you're feeling good with where you are on your journey. More importantly, you're feeling good with who you are as a person. If you feel a deep sense of sadness, or you actually struggle to look at yourself at all, you might want to take some time to sit for a while, and ask yourself why?

Once you learn to trust yourself, and really to know who you are inside, then you will start to trust in other things such as the signs around you and how you interpret them for yourself. You will know because you will feel trust, and how it resonates inside your body. It might feel as if you've discovered a huge secret and you will not be able to stop smiling.

All of your actions, from then on, will be guided towards keeping this feeling, which comes from knowing the truth of your soul. Staying in spirit will become second nature and doing the work of spirit will be the only role you want.

*****

As an example, imagine you go out to a club because your favourite singer is appearing. But, you have a really bad cold and you've lost your hearing. You're at the club and the singer begins their first song. You know they are singing because you can see that they are, but you cannot hear them. Can you say 100% that they were truly singing? Crazy analogy, but go with me.

A week later, your hearing has cleared up. However, during the week it was extremely windy and you got some foreign matter in your eyes. It has been treated by the doctor but you have to keep the bandages on over the weekend. Your friends decide to take you out to a club to cheer you up. You're happy to be there, as you love live music. The singer begins their set. The music is amazing and sounds just as it does on their record, but you can't see them. Can you say 100% that it was that person playing live? Is there room for doubt?

What happens when you go back to the same club, after your eyes and ears are back to normal? You can see and hear everything perfectly. How do you feel? Does this experience feel different from the other two? Do you feel you can absolutely trust what you're hearing and seeing? I'm guessing your answer is yes! Why do you think this is? Maybe it is because of the fact that you've been using those two senses together your whole life and it is second nature for you to trust them implicitly.

Now, you're at the same club and you notice that one of the people sitting at the table near you is blind. After your earlier experiences, you ask yourself, how they can get a true appreciation of the show without being able to see it. They have never had the gift of sight, so they've used their other senses, to a deeper level than you or I might have, which provides them with a different level of appreciation of what they are experiencing. There are so many small nuances in the way they navigate their world, so that they become more aware of their surroundings because of their need to do so.

So, who trusts their sixth sense, their intuition, more? Some people's intuition kicks in very early, others much later, and some may never use it at all. But, each person's truth is their own, just as each person's parameters for trusting are uniquely their own.

So how do you trust it? Who will you trust? The sooner you know you can trust yourself the sooner you will be able to trust in your intuition and the sooner it will become second nature for you.

"Truth Resurrected,
Understood,
Supported, and Treasured."

CHAPTER 20

Victorious

What happens in between these pages is, in part, my experience of how I learnt to trust myself again, to be able to function and hopefully to excel at life, and at living. The more true I was to myself the less I felt I had to tippy toe around what others thought I was, or should be, and the fewer 'eggshells' I walked on in the process.

By this, I mean that when you try to be what others want you to be, or how you think you're supposed to be, it's like trying to walk down a pavement and not step on the lines. Eventually you're going to step on a line or two, crack an eggshell or three, or disappoint someone. If you remain true to who you are, then eventually the people around you will either accept you or they won't. Being able to step away from any situation emotionally, allows you to focus on what is right for you.

I got the chance to witness how far I'd come from, where I'd been, once, when I was picking up the children from a weekend visit. As I walked across the street to where they were, I heard the children yelling out. "Daddy hurt his back."

The closer I got the more visible his pain became. I walked straight up to him and reached out to hold him. It was a moment outside of time, and outside of my life. Through compassion and love all I saw was a soul in pain, anguish etched in his eyes and pain tormenting his body.

I held him in my arms, acknowledging his pain and his commitment to our soul journey together as well as the love we'd once shared, and still did somewhere in time.

My human self asked, "How could I?"

My soul said, "How could I not?"

Time became linear again and we moved away from each other and back into our physical lives.

When our actions come without thought, and from kindness and compassion, there can be nothing else. No victim, no giving our power away, only an exchange of energy that benefits both the giver and the receiver.

Learning things the way I have was hard and I'm sure no harder than some of the things you've also gone through in your life. However, it is like anything you do in life. The more you practice the better you become at it. Some people even go on to be experts in their chosen field, wherever their specific talent takes them. Some we hear about; extraordinary athletes, Oscar winning actors, and doctors, the list goes on.

Then, there are those we don't hear about, such as the corner grocer who has customers coming back week after week, year after year, because people can feel when someone loves what they do. They have a great energy around them and people want to be around that energy. They are champions in their lives. Again, where compassion and love exist nothing else can.

I hope that you've found something you can use in these pages, to help you grow your life into one that fills you with excitement and joy. A life that makes you jump out of bed joyfully in the morning, because you're happy with who you are and in the life you chose, as well as the direction your life is heading. Are you in love with your life, and in love with yourself? How do you know if you are? Oh, you will know! I promise, you will know, and it starts with your opinion of yourself being the one that matters most.

Believing in yourself will take you further than self-doubt, any day of the week!

Feel the excitement within, when no one else is around! For me, this is writing and sharing what I know, hoping it may be of help to others. It is swimming in the ocean, or an ocean pool, when I'm the only one there to witness the light, smell, and texture of a new day. It is to witness the sound of my son's laughter, or see the smile on my daughter's face or the joy on my granddaughter's face when they are not aware I see these things. This is my bliss and my heart is full to overflowing!

*****

Throughout my life, the only time I've felt truly on purpose was when I was giving readings to those who came to me. Whether it was in a workshop, through a reading, or even a casual conversation, this was (and is) when the energy flows through my body. The words I speak, and the things I see during this time come from some other place. This is when my mind and thoughts move aside to free the space for something pure and powerful to come through. I give out information that I didn't know, for the person sitting with me, for whom it was meant. It has become such an integral and sacred part of me over the years. It is as natural as breathing.

The studies I undertook throughout my life, and not all in the classroom, seem to have been a necessary and integral part of my learning and growth, until I could embrace all that I am without question. We may call it by different names. I call it the God source within, the infinite soul presence that guides me, and that guides each one of us towards the life we chose, and were meant to live.

It is the one, who answers if we call. It is the one, who knows the answer to every question we ever have. It is the voice we hear, when we ask for guidance. I believe it doesn't matter what we call it; only that we know and embrace it.

I hope I've helped to answer some of the questions you may have had. I hope some of what we've talked about here, helps you to stay open, not only to your own reality but also to the reality of others. More than anything, I hope what we've shared here keeps you asking questions about yourself, until you find the fulfilment you desire in living your most inspired life.

"We come from the Rainbow Pool of Light.
We birth into our package of choice
learning, in the playground called Earth.
It is a game we play,
to learn and discover feelings,
and to know and absorb them as a physical being,
in the time of now,
as those in The Rainbow Pool of Light watch on..."

CHAPTER 21

Choosing the Space

Choose a space for half an hour, half a day, or half a lifetime. Which did you choose? There is something for you to find in 'the space' if you allow.

You don't need anything, but some uninterrupted time and a place where you feel calm and safe. Your intuition, your sixth sense is waiting for you, and longing for you to come and claim it back into your life. Do you have a space in your home? If so, keep a writing pad and pen there for you to write down any thoughts, images, or things you might get during your time there.

Maybe you like walking in nature or floating in the ocean pool, or swimming in the ocean. It only has to be somewhere where you know you can be alone for about fifteen minutes, to start.

The important thing is to make a commitment to yourself. Allow some time each day, to be open to making this connection. You will be more likely to do it, if you can integrate it into your daily routine. Otherwise, get up fifteen minutes earlier or take fifteen minutes at the end of your day. You will need to set your intention. Write it down, if possible. Otherwise just say it aloud. If you don't know what to write or say, think of the first thing you need help with or would like to be able to do. Maybe it could be as simple as asking for help to make sure you have an extra fifteen minutes to be in this space every day.

Simplistic? Of course, but that's what using your intuition is all about. It's about helping to make your life a lot simpler, so you feel freer. The next step is about breathing.

Learn to breathe deeply and slowly, in and out, so that all your focus is on your breath. The idea is to clear conscious thoughts from your mind, to allow space for your intuition – your spiritual self – to talk to you.

You will recognise these types of thought. They are very clear and short, rather like an idea that just pops into your head out of nowhere and may appear to be totally random. If it doesn't happen straight away. keep at it. If you haven't attempted anything like this before, it may take a little while for you to get the hang of it. If you really want this, don't give up.

Find any tools that work for you, and there are plenty out there. Use your intuition to select the one or ones you feel drawn to the most. Sometimes you may just *know* they are right, and other times they might surprise you. Just for fun, I've put in a list of some of the kinds of things that could work for you. What I would like you to do is to get a pen and paper and write down the following list. Then find a store in your local area, or city and have a look around in that store.

Items

- ☐ *Crystals*
- ☐ *Runes*
- ☐ *Tarot cards*
- ☐ *Other card decks*
- ☐ *Pendulums*
- ☐ *Tea cup readings*
- ☐ *Books*
- ☐ *Books on dreams*
- ☐ *Books on signs*
- ☐ *Maybe you come across a **feather**, a **flower**, a **leaf** on your travels*

The list is endless.

Then, tick the first one you're drawn to on your list.

Next, write down what appeals to you about the object or book you've ticked.

Now, pick up any of the things in the shop that you might feel drawn to. I imagine that many of you will have done this at least once, but if not, I hope you will enjoy it. If you select crystals, ask the person in the shop what it/they mean. I guarantee it will be something where you say, "Oh my gosh. This is such a coincidence."

But what do I always say? "There are no coincidences!"

Regardless what it is, ask the shop person about it. They really love explaining about whatever it is they have that may interest you, and they never try to pressure you into buying anything.

Then, later on that evening, sit in your quiet space. If you did get something you were drawn to earlier, hold it. Hold an image of it in your mind and just allow any thoughts to come and go through your mind, until they stop or until you feel you want to stop.

Either way, it might only be for about fifteen minutes. If it turns out to be longer, that's good too. After you've opened your eyes, write down anything that came through your mind, anything at all. Your note pad will act as a diary. Keep doing this for about a week, and then go back and reread everything you've written.

*****

To explain what I mean further, let me share an example with you. I was at the airport in February this year, 2020, going to the Gold Coast. I ventured back again, a month later on some business and came home on Friday 13th March 2020. Despite everything that has happened this year I still think of Friday 13th as a very lucky day. I always have and I don't buy into the superstition around it.

Anyway, two things happened between the trips I took. On the Thursday night before I flew home I heard that two American actors had tested positive for Covid-19. The day after I arrived home, the world we had known slowly started to disappear as the virus took hold.

The second thing that happened was this. As I was walking through the airport towards the plane to come home, I stopped. I felt something pulling me back to the newsagent's I had just walked past. I turned around trusting there was a reason for this and began walking back. This time, I actually entered the store, so I could see what I had walked past. Straight away, I saw it on a stand of books. I immediately knew it was meant to be mine. I reached out and picked it up and I felt as if it had been mine forever.

It was the most exquisite set of cards, (Rebecca Campbell, 2018). Not exactly Tarot cards but in a similar vein. What had drawn me to them was light; a magnificent, powerful light that glowed from them. What is funny is that I haven't even thought about buying any cards for many years, and yet this pack made its way to me. I might also say that there was only one pack and I've never seen them anywhere since. Weird, Crazy? Maybe yes, maybe no.

A coincidence! Ha! I don't think so. What I also found interesting about these cards was they were different to the earthy feeling of the Tarot decks. These cards feel celestial and the light that emanates from them is spellbinding.

Pardon the pun. Can anyone else see what I see in them? No, they can't. Oh, they think they are beautiful but no light, nothing. Was I imagining it? No I wasn't.

I feel I've gotten to a place where I have or can find the peace I seek, even when my world is swirling around me, as it continues to do. Although, I must admit, I have been tested way above my limits these past few weeks and I have no shame in admitting I have struggled, am struggling, to find the peace I seek in this moment.

Deep breathing and meditation are the tools I use to get to the space where I can access my inner self. It is an ever evolving process. As I continue to embrace the things I've learnt along the way, I feel more and more able to let go and to allow this beautiful process, we call life, to evolve into the rare and unique flower it is. This is what I hope you have or will find for you.

Your world takes on a whole new meaning, once you feel the confidence that comes when you remember what you bought to share with others. You will feel lighter, as though a heavy weight has been lifted off and you could run forever. This is what happens. This is how it feels when you find the purpose you've been waiting to find, although I think a better word here is *'remember'*. You have finally allowed yourself to wake up to the knowledge you brought to share.

Some people know this already, from a very young age, but most of us don't. It might take many life lessons, finally, for us to remember what our special gift is. When you remember, it isn't really a surprise at all, because it confirms something you've felt inside you but could never really give a name to; until now. However it comes to you, embrace it openly and honestly. You will love yourself for it.

Although there may always be *thorns* and *speed bumps* throughout life, I try to minimise their impact, and the pain and the damage they can cause, by slowing down, breathing, and allowing life to flow. All the while I stay centred, knowing that all is as it should be and that life does not revolve around me, but through me. I'm only one small particle of the whole beautiful experience.

I live a normal life, just as you do, if any life can be called normal. I have decisions to make, and choices to choose, and not all of them will end up perfect. This is a fact of life. However, the more information you have beforehand, helps you make the right choice for you, at the right time. Sometimes, my choices weave around like a road map without a destination in mind, but I follow them, because I feel good each step of the way. Eventually, when I arrive, I know this is exactly where I imagined I would be. Sometimes my feelings about where I think I'm going change, a little like the children's game 'Hot and Cold' that I play with my granddaughter.

Wouldn't it be wonderful if we had someone who could call out like this for us? Well we do! It is our own guidance system. Our internal GPS, our intuition, our gut reaction, our faith! Whatever you call it, it is always with you. All we need to do is to ask for guidance and then, listen. Because the very next choice you make could end up being the most exciting and surprising choice of your life!

Learning from my mistakes – and there have been plenty – is what keeps me wanting to learn even more. I want to keep learning for the rest of my life, because learning is mind opening for me, and learning is growing and moving forward. I'm not saying that all the lessons have been fun, far from it. In the learning stage, it can also be emotional, confusing and even fearful. However, when I move from learning to understanding, I feel hope. This is the part I truly love. It is so empowering! I become freer and more opportunities open up for me, because I've stopped placing limits on my thoughts. Those limits were not placed there by me, not consciously anyway, but by someone else a long time ago. Once I began sitting quietly in the moments of life and listening, I found understanding came.

Only then, could I see further than my next step. Maybe these opportunities were always there and I just hadn't been open to seeing them. After you learn to trust in yourself and what you feel, it becomes easier to make choices, big choices, small choices it doesn't matter. The important thing is to make them. Don't allow yourself to be paralysed by the fear of making the wrong choice. Every choice keeps you moving forward in your life. If it feels right at the time, then in that moment it becomes the only choice you can make. The only wrong choice is no choice at all.

*****

I spent years feeling less than I was, and making choices, learning from them and then making more choices, all the while learning and embracing the knowledge I was gaining. Only then did I come to understand the one thing I had been missing all along.

I was not '*deserving*' of love. No! By making choice after choice, with only healing and goodness in my heart, I realised what some already know and what some may never learn. We don't need to *try, we don't need to do, and we don't need to be more,* to deserve love. We only need to know that we *are* love.

Stand tall in the knowledge and truth of who you are. For you and I are **Pure Divine Beings of Love**!

What I can say is that, yes it is nice to feel love and appreciation from those in our life whom we love; our family, our friends, and those we work with. However, if their opinion of you is how you define your self-worth, I can almost guarantee you will not feel strong. Why? Because the opinions of others are always moving and changing. True self-worth, and self-love comes from inside and the certainty of that knowledge is always carried in your heart. You only need to trust it, believe it, and know it.

*****

"Joy leaves,
When I allow others to define me.
Yet, I am unique and in being so
cannot be defined by others,
but only by my own perceptions."

*****

When someone is in pain, they cannot see much else. Life is all about their pain, my pain, or your pain. At these times, these people may lash out at others. We need to move through the pain in order to be able to function again. When my children were small, and they came home from school telling me how someone had hurt them physically or verbally, and sometimes both, I would take it up with the school principal for obvious reasons. However, I always sat my children down and we talked about possible reasons why it may have happened.

"If someone hurts you and you know you haven't done anything to provoke it, I want you to think about it. Try to imagine just how much pain they must be in to hurt someone else like that." Except for the 'normal' teenager problems, I never had to address this issue with them again. Children understand much more than we know or give them credit for.

This was one of the most important lessons that I learnt. If someone hurts you, it is the pain that is important. Sometimes, pain is how we learn. Our thoughts are extremely powerful and maybe just what those in pain need to begin their own journey back to love.

We must all take responsibility for our own pain and whether we choose to fix it or not. We must want to fix our pain, but some people don't want to, or don't know how to. Being open to it is the first step. When you trust that part of you, you can see many doorways and not just the one you're standing in. Sometimes, the things that change us most are the things we don't see coming.

I'm not sure I would want to, either. Oh, you might have a *feeling* that something is going to happen. A premonition, your intuition, or your instincts are telling you one thing, but you may decide to do the exact opposite anyway.

Our choices define us. I love the person I am today! I also hope you love the person you have become through your choices. If you're not quite there yet, don't worry because you will get there. It might happen in the very next choice you make for yourself. So have faith in your intuition, your gut instincts, hunches or faith, because I have faith in you.

*"Faith is
the force
of life."*

Leo Tolstoy

Should I have made different choices along the way? Maybe! It certainly might have seemed a lot easier to do and who knows where different choices would have led? But, I don't want even to try to imagine what my life would be without my children and my beautiful granddaughter, whom I love beyond expression. I cannot imagine my life without the friends I have because of my choices along the way, OR indeed, the person I have become.

As crazy as it sounds I love all of the choices I made and I've come to love all the pain too. That pain pushed me to make the choices I did. Love pushed me to believe in myself as a complete human being and a spiritual being enmeshed into one. Embracing and loving my whole self, on every level of my being, and trusting in the higher order of things has helped to get me to where I am now.

Have you ever experienced one of those moments, where you feel as if it has all happened before? When, as it's happening, you already know what is going to be said and what is going to happen? It can be as simple as talking to a friend and all of a sudden, you *know* you've already been here and done exactly the same. Sometimes you might even say "This has happened before."

This is called **déjà vu**. Now you may or may not already know this. I believe that these moments tell me that I'm on track. I'm on the right path in my journey through this life. They are reminders that my life is unfolding as it should, and that I'm on my path to completing the reason I came into this life.

Would I want to know the exact moment things are about to happen? What would be the fun in that? However, trusting and having absolute faith that I will get through, whatever life brings my way, and that I don't have to do it alone is the greatest gift – the greatest joy. Trusting my intuition, listening to the God within and my inner guidance system, and allowing that inner GPS to guide me to where I need to be, has given me a life full of the highest highs and, yes, the lowest lows. It has brought my deepest despair and my ultimate feelings of joy and love. Would I have wanted some things to be different? Absolutely. When I was in the middle of it!

Though from where I stand today, I can look back and see my life was the most perfect life for me and the choices I made were the most perfect I could have made. As I said before, hindsight is a wonderful thing.

I hope I never make it to the top of my mountain, at least not yet anyway. I want to keep learning. I want to keep growing and embracing whatever life has in store for me. However, when the time eventually comes – as it does for all living beings... know Mum and Dad and all those I've loved and lost will be waiting for me on the other side of that *doorway*, wherever that doorway is. I will step through joyfully, because my time here will have been fulfilled. "*The Circle of Life*" will continue through my children and their children. This is life and what a beautiful life it is.

*"The best
and most beautiful things in the world
cannot be seen or even touched
- they must be felt with the heart."*

Helen Keller

CHAPTER 22

Honesty

Sometimes, when I'm writing and I look at what I've written, I feel as though it paints a picture of someone who has it all together. I can assure you I absolutely am not that person. I make mistakes, sometimes many mistakes. I may not listen to my intuition, especially if I'm having a bad day.

For instance, this morning is, was, my Mum's birthday and I had just arrived at work. It was still early and no customers had come in, so I wanted to put up a picture of Mum on my Instagram page, to honour her and her day. However, when I tried to do so, I found there were no pictures of Mum in my phone.

My phone had died a couple of months ago and I needed to buy a new one. Technology and I have a struggling relationship, to which many of my friends will attest. So, I had not actually realised there was a cloud somewhere where I could save photos, which is rather ironic because Mum is way above the clouds now, anyway. The point is they were not there on my new phone when I wanted to upload one.

Grief tore away my composure and I had to walk into the back office and get all my tears out in one go, instead of sitting in my chair feeling them slide down my face one by one. Not an attractive look I can assure you but at least, then I could function professionally for our customers when they did come in.

It has been a really tough few years for me leading up to 2020, and then Covid-19 hit with the slow building power of a tidal wave, sucking the life out of our lives. Our lives became like something we had only ever seen in the movies. There were even movies coming out on our screens to remind us of this, at the time.

Watching as pictures of our world flashed over all media outlets with not a soul about reminded me of an old movie that was remade with Keanu Reeves, called 'The Day the Earth Stood Still' (2008). On the news, capital cities were eerily empty, as in the film where the earth fell quiet with a serene cover of fear. I remember how much the original version terrified me as a little girl. Now all we can do in our 'new world' is to isolate, while we wait for another update.

I am, and have always been, a hugging-kind of person. I've found it quite surreal not being able to hug anyone. It reminds me of a notice that goes around, once in a while, which says how important it is to hug someone; really hug someone, for both of you. It is right up there with water, as a requirement for our very survival.

Watching someone's face after they've received a hug gives me so much joy. They appear to light up from the inside. A hug cost nothing and can give a person a feeling of connection, love, kindness, gratitude, and hopefulness. It is ironic that one tiny virus can deprive so many of so much. What this virus has reinforced in me is how important family is and that family is not just this family or that family, but our entire family, as human beings, inhabiting our home called Earth.

This chapter is about honesty. So what did isolation do to me and for me this past year? It upped my anxiety levels. It meant my depression needed more help than I could get alone. Even a trip to the shopping centre was crazy, trying to navigate through the people in the supermarket. Some were sticking to the Covid-19 distancing rules, and wearing masks etc. Then, there were those who didn't care at all and were pushing past the rest of us.

I got to the point where, anytime I needed supplies, I felt as although my body was getting small electric shocks if a person came near me or actually bumped into me.

Asking for help, when it was so obvious I needed it, was a choice I had no difficulty making. That choice and getting the help I needed saved me. It also helped me get to the underlying cause of what was actually pushing my buttons, so to speak. Asking for help is hard, especially when I had spent years trying to do everything myself.

I used to think that if I muddled through on my own, it made me stronger and I felt capable of looking after my family and myself. However as I've discovered, no one person is capable of doing everything. Having friends and people around who care and give me support, when I need it, makes me feel very humble, very human and very loved.

My prayer is for a post Covid-19 world where we are kinder, and more caring and compassionate towards each other and to ourselves; to our world, our planet, and our home. I pray for a world where we stand together as one family. I pray that now, we as a people, know and understand the pain and suffering caused by isolation we rally to remove isolation from our society.

I brought my children up, telling them not to be scared of asking for help if they needed it, or of saying, I don't understand when you don't. I encouraged them to ask questions. It takes courage to do these things and, believe it or not, the majority of people around you probably don't know the answers either. Be the one who steps up. Be brave and be your authentic self.

For me, being psychic does not negate me from being human. Far from it; it makes me feel even more human, if that is possible? It allows me to know myself from the inside out and the inside is where we all hide our hurt, our love... and our truth.

"Once you embrace your truth!
Once you embrace all that you are!
Once you express yourself without fear!
Once you express the soul centre of who you are!

And, once you express your gift,
that gift you brought to share!
Your world becomes exquisite!

For you stand at the centre of the universe!
You stand as its creator!
Create! Expand! Be!
Be the space you want to live in!"

*****

One thing that using my intuition, to the extent I have, has taught me, is this. There is a time in the early morning, somewhere between 03:30am and 05:30am, where the outside world is quiet. I relish sitting in the quiet stillness with my tea, note pad, and pen. All thoughts of the relevant and irrelevant things in my life fall away. As I sit, a peaceful calm moves through my body and mind. It is the time of day that I love the most. The world slips away and yet I'm filled with a deep connection to all things and peace is the place where we sit together.

I wish I could stay there forever and some days it feels as if I do, when the writing flows. Before I know it the day has disappeared and night descends. I feel such joy in this shared connection. On other days, I swim in the ocean, watching the sunrise above the horizon. I am alone in the water and yet, knowing how connected I am to all things, this fills me with peace and a serene calm.

"*Here!*
Floating!
Held within time
No more separate from it!
I am timeless, and my small life
takes on a whole new meaning…"

*****

All any of us wish for is to feel that connection, to feel connected and to feel heard. We spend our lives in search of this connection in relationships, in substances and in activities, but this searching is always outside of ourselves.

We're looking for someone or something that will provide us with that feeling of being connected. However, when that relationship ends or that substance or activity is beyond our reach, we feel disconnected.

For me the truest connection I've found is not to someone or something. It is within. It was by learning to trust my intuitive nature. By following that guidance, I've found peace within, and within this peace I found the gift of myself.

Now you may say, 'That is crazy. Of course, we need others. We need to function in the world around us and share love with our family, our friends.' I would say to you this: 'Absolutely, this is most definitely true!'

However, what I'm actually saying is this; when you've no need to seek out others... when you are *all* to yourself... when you realise and embrace that *you ARE* the connection you seek... then all these other relationships change. They change into rare and exquisite birds, ones that you don't need to hang onto to feel the connection.

You don't need to hold them tightly because it is not *them;* it is not the *other* you need. *You* are what you've been searching for! Your entire special, unique, and beautiful self. There is no one on this earth who can give you this gift but you. This knowledge gives you an appreciation of everything and everyone as nothing else can.

My journey, my *road trip* to know myself has had many twists and turns, but the real catalyst that pushed me to unwrap, discover, and learn more about my psychic spiritual self was this.

Somewhere deep inside, I knew there was more to me than the tattered threads of a broken marriage. There was more to me than the fragile, fear-filled woman I had become. I knew that if I trusted this feeling, I would find the strength I needed to move my family and myself forward. So, I began taking step-by-step action when action was needed and, over the years I learnt not to look towards tomorrow.

The only thing I could count on was the moment I was in. So while things around me moved swiftly, e.g., selling our home, finding somewhere new and safe for us to live, I kept moving from moment to moment.

I felt a great sense of accomplishment, after I'd moved my children, our dog, and myself from one end of Sydney to the other – to Palm Beach – and into our first home together as a new kind of family. I witnessed the joy and excitement on the faces of my children, as they ran freely through our home choosing which room they would make their own, and heard their unbridled laughter. I felt the need to become a better person, a better mother, and a more complete human and spiritual being – for them, and more importantly for myself!

What's that saying?

> " If you love someone, set them free.
> If they come back they're ours;
> If they don't they never were."

Richard Bach

We cannot *own* another living being. We can only be their caretakers – even of the children who come through us – until they can fly on their own, *AND* this is my wish for each one of you.

That you all learn to FLY and may your light support your wings!

I think back to when I was sitting on Avalon Beach and the wind gifted me a wish, but I was too afraid I'd screw it up to make it. I was afraid I didn't deserve what my heart longed for; afraid I'd done so many things wrong that I didn't know how to do it right.

Now, I understand that by actually having the courage to make my wish; well, that was my chance to be honest with myself, even if only for that one small moment and that being honest with myself was the only place I could begin to believe again, to begin again!

Don't be afraid as I was. Don't wait to make your wishes come true. Take the leap! Make the wish! *JUMP!!!*

This book and the people I've had the honour of helping along the way was/is, my *wish*...

AFTERWORD

As I sit here in this year of 2021, I find that life has come full circle again. Today, I lost my best friend. In a way it was sudden and much too quick for those of us who loved you. You were my sister in every meaning of the word. You were part of my daily routine, whether it be a phone call and a cup of tea or a swim and breakfast by the sea. To say I will miss you seems ridiculously small. To say you will be missed by many is the craziest understatement of them all.

You have tested my beliefs, though I still hold them true and I am expecting, at least, one 'visit' from you.

*****

Just now, as I walked outside to breathe in the new day I saw it. Tucked away in between the flowers and a wall was a small white and black feather that had not been there before.

Our angels are never far, always giving 100% of their knowledge, strength, love, and support. Now there's a new one in the fold. And, whether it's a father from beyond or a friend with just the right word or two have no doubt! They ARE here, with a hand on your shoulder, letting you know they are with you and it will Always be so.

"When your heart is open wide,
others will be able to do that, too.
For there are many out there, just like you.
So share your heart, do not hide,
Be your light… Step outside… and,
SHINE!!!"

THANK YOU

Lessons... wish to thank all the teachers, throughout my life, for lessons that helped me grow and gain knowledge, through pain and through love. Most of you probably didn't know this at the time, but then, neither did I. We honoured the contracts, and promises we made to each other somewhere in the ether before our arrival; before our birth. Sitting here at my desk, now, I feel incredibly blessed and enormously grateful for the roles you played in my story; my journey.

Family - Thank you to my children. No mother could be more blessed or feel more honoured that you chose me to learn from and to teach. Thank you for showing me the infinite levels of love that exist. Thank you for reminding me how resolutely strong a heart can be and how much a heart can hold as well as what unconditional love truly is. Your being here reminds me what is truly important and I've tried to respect your privacy as much as possible.

During the last fifteen years of his life, my dad showed me how burnt bridges can open the way for more love, more understanding and can allow compassion to come into your life. In these past few years, I've come to know the true meaning of *family* and that love is never late. Our lives can be busy in the day-to-day roles we play, but family is always there, just waiting for the right moment and the right timing to blossom again, and again. Thank you to my big beautiful family for showing up in my life.

Friends... am so grateful to have the kinds of friends I have. Without your love and support, I doubt I could have got this far. Thank you seems so small a word to encompass the love and gratitude I feel for my female friends. Each of you have a special place in my heart and without you I would not be me; I could not be me. You walk beside me, gifts, filled with encouragement, compassion, love, and support. You even give me a kick in the behind when you know I need one. The girl friends I call my sisters. How would I ever get through without you? You know who you are, and more importantly, I know who you are.

To my editor, thank you for the finishing touches to help make it something special. To the production team, and to everyone involved in the many processes of getting my manuscript published. I am so grateful to you, each one of you.

I thank my sixth sense, intuition, timing, and learning how to trust again.

What can I say about Rachael, my mentor? Without you, my book would still be a dream... my *wish*, with notes, short stories and the like sitting in the corner of my office. You have shared your enthusiasm with me and given me your time and professionalism, all the while making me feel like a friend. You sliced through my self-doubt and kept me on track. I am so grateful you decided to pick up the phone when I reached out!!!

RECOMMENDED READING

Sonia Choquetta, *Ask Your Guides*, Revised Edition, Published by Hay House Australia Pty. Ltd, Australia, 2021

Dr. Wayne W Dyer, *Living an Inspired Life – Your Ultimate Calling*, Published by Hay House, USA 2016

Barry Eaton, *Past Lives Unveiled*, Published by Rockpool Publishing, Australia, 2019

Kyle Gray, *Angel Numbers*, Published by Hay House Australia Ltd., Australia, 2019

Judy Hall, *The Crystal Bible*, Published by Walking Stick Press USA, 2003

Louise Hay, *Do Your Mirror Work*, Published by Hay House USA, 1984

Louise Hay, *You Can Heal Your Life*, Published by Hay House Australia Pty. Ltd, 1999

Chris Mackey, *The Positive Psychology of Synchronicity*, Published by Watkins, an imprint of Watkins Media Limited, UK and USA 2015, 2019

Phillip Permutt, *The Crystal Healer*, Published by CICO Books an imprint of Ryland Peters & Small Ltd., London, New York, 2016

Dr. David A. Phillips, *Discovering the Inner Self, The Complete Book of Numerology*, Published by Gary Allen Pty Ltd Australia, 1992

Gilly Pickup, *The Little Book of Meditations*, Published by Summersdale Publishers Ltd., London UK, 2019

D. Virtue & L Brown, *Angel Numbers*, Published by Hay House Australia Pty. Ltd, 2005

CARD DECKS

Rebecca Campbell, Artwork by Danielle Noel, *Work Your Light*, Oracle Cards, Published by Hay House Australia Ltd., 2018

Alexis Cartwright, *Transference Healing Animal Magic*, Ascension Cards, Published by Transference Healing Pty. Ltd., Australia, 2nd Edition, 2018

James Wanless, PhD., Artwork by Ken Knutson, *VOYAGER Tarot*, Published by Merrill-West Publishing, USA, 1986, 1998 2nd Edition

426

BIBLIOGRAPHY

Rachael Bermingham. *Savvy*, Published by Hay House Australia Pty Ltd. 2012

Rebecca Campbell, Artwork by Danielle Noel, *Work Your Light*, Oracle Cards, Published by Hay House Australia Ltd., 2018

Deepak Chopra, *You Can Heal Your Life* - Seminar, Horden Pavilion, Sydney Australia, 1998

William Dear, Director, *Angels in the Outfield,* Production Co.; Walt Disney Pictures, Caravan Pictures, USA, 1994 (remake of original 1951 film)

Scott Derrickson, Director, *The Day the Earth Stood Still,* Production Co.; 3 Arts Entertainment, Dune Entertainment USA, 2008 (loose adaptation of original 1951 film)

Wayne W. Dyer, *You Can Heal Your Life* - Seminar, Horden Pavilion, Sydney Australia, 1998

Louise Hay, *Do Your Mirror Work,* Published by Hay House USA, 1984

Kinsley Jarrett, *Visions of the Ascended Masters,* Published by SPIRAL Australia, 1992

Elton John, Composer, Tim Rice, Lyricist, *Circle of Life,* The Lion King: Original Motion Picture Soundtrack, Recorded Santa Monica, USA 1993

Lionel Richie, Mike Frenchie, and Carlos Rios Writers, *Dancing on the Ceiling* Producer Richie, Carmichael, Walden for Perfect Light Productions USA 1986

Karen N Sawyer, *A Window in Time*, Published by Teiaiel Publications Australia, 2000

Neale Donald Walsh, *The Little Soul and the Sun*, Published by Hampton Roads Publishing Company Inc. 1998

James Wanless, PH.D., Artwork by Ken Knutson, *VOYAGER Tarot*, Published by Merrill-West Publishing, USA, 1986, 1998 2nd Edition

Jerry Zucker, Director, *Ghost*, Production Co.; Paramount Pictures Howard W. Koch Productions, USA, 1990

BIOGRAPHY

Karen wrote her first book, a poetry book called *A Window in Time* (2000), soon after moving to the northern beaches of Sydney with her children. After some unexpected events, her writing had to be put on hold, *although not with Spirit,* as family and other commitments took priority.

She became a volunteer lifesaver at Avalon Beach and spent a lot of time there, when her children were young, revelling in the healthy outdoor lifestyle it provided.

Karen N Sawyer

At the same time, she decided to expand her writing skills further by taking on a Degree in Literature at Macquarie University. It seemed however, the universe had other ideas, and Karen took on a filler subject, in cultural studies during her second year. She decided to make that her major as she found it fascinating.

This opened up her world even more and it became very important in expanding the ideals she lives by as a spiritual, human being further. This in turn also enhanced her psychic work in deeper and even more fulfilling ways. This work led Karen to her next role, working at a local football club for over ten wonderful years.

Karen also loved talking with local community groups on subjects that were important to them and to her. Her work as a funeral director enabled her to grow in her understanding of the things people placed importance on when a love one passes.

She found that although we all may have different rituals, regarding the process of death, we still process our pain and humanity the same. When this is tempered with humility and compassion, it allows us to cross any bridge that separates us, so that we finally stand together in spirit and love as brothers and sisters.

An avid reader, Karen loves catching up on the latest books. and films are a must-do during holiday breaks. Casual catch-ups with family and a close group of girl friends fill her life with joy.

Favourite Spot: Narrabeen Ocean Pool

What's Next: Maybe another road trip, who knows? One thing I've learnt for sure is that nothing is sure. So what's next? That would be wherever life, the universe, or the wind takes me. Wherever I am meant to be... I will be.

MAKING CONTACT

Karen can be contacted through:

Website: www.Karennsawyer.com
Email: Karen.sawyer88@gmail.com
Facebook: Karen N Sawyer
Instagram: Karennsawyer

CPSIA information can be obtained
at www.ICGtesting.com
Printed in the USA
BVHW050541040821
613604BV00016B/358